D0519995

The New Encyclopedia of Crochet Techniques

CALGARY PUBLIC LIBRARY

DEC - - 2012

The New Encyclopedia of Crochet Techniques

A comprehensive visual guide to traditional and contemporary techniques

Jan Eaton

RUNNING PRESS
PHILADELPHIA · LONDON

A QUARTO BOOK

Copyright © 2006 & 2012 Quarto Inc.
First published in the United States in 2012 by
Running Press Book Publishers
A Member of the Perseus Books Group

All rights reserved under the Pan-American and
International Copyright Conventions
Color separation in Singapore by Pica Digital Pte Ltd
Printed in China by 1010 Printing International Ltd

This book may not be reproduced in whole or in part, in any
form or by any means, electronic or mechanical, including
photocopying, recording, or by any information storage and
retrieval system now known or hereafter invented, without
written permission from the publisher.

Books published by Running Press are available at special
discounts for bulk purchases in the United States by
corporations, institutions, and other organizations. For more
information, please contact the Special Markets Department
at the Perseus Books Group, 2300 Chestnut Street, Suite 200,
Philadelphia, PA 19103, or call (800) 810-4145, ext. 5000, or
e-mail special.markets@perseusbooks.com.

ISBN: 978-0-7624-4749-7
Library of Congress Control Number: 2012938528

9 8 7 6 5 4 3 2 1
Digit on the right indicates the number of this printing

Conceived, designed, and produced by
Quarto Publishing plc
The Old Brewery
6 Blundell Street
London N7 9BH

QUA: ECR2

PROJECT EDITOR: Lindsay Kaubi
ART EDITOR: Julie Francis
COPY EDITORS: Pauline Hornsby, Helen Jordan
ILLUSTRATORS: Betty Barnden, Kuo Kang Chen, Coral Mula
PHOTOGRAPHERS: Martin Norris, Phil Wilkins
PICTURE RESEARCHERS: Sarah Bell, Claudia Tate

CREATIVE DIRECTOR: Moira Clinch
PUBLISHER: Paul Carslake

Running Press Book Publishers
2300 Chestnut Street
Philadelphia, PA 19103-4371

Visit us on the web!
www.runningpress.com

CONTENTS

ABOUT THIS BOOK

THE BOOK BEGINS WITH CROCHET ESSENTIALS, A CHAPTER PACKED WITH THE BASICS OF CROCHET. ONCE YOU HAVE MASTERED THE BASICS, MOVE ON TO THE TECHNIQUES AND STITCHES CHAPTER, WHICH WILL EXPAND YOUR KNOWLEDGE AND SKILLS. EACH TECHNIQUE IS SELF-CONTAINED, SO YOU CAN EITHER DIP IN AND OUT OF THE CHAPTER OR WORK YOUR WAY FROM BEGINNING TO END. THE PROJECTS AND GALLERY CHAPTERS ARE INTENDED TO ENCOURAGE YOU TO PUT INTO PRACTICE THE SKILLS YOU HAVE LEARNED.

CROCHET ESSENTIALS

Crochet Essentials guides you step-by-step through all the crochet basics in easy-to-follow sequences, progressing from equipment and materials and how to hold the hook and yarn to basic stitches, how to read patterns, and how to stitch seams. This course in the essentials will direct you through your first steps in crochet.

Step-by-step sequences and clear, easy-to-follow illustrations accompany each skill.

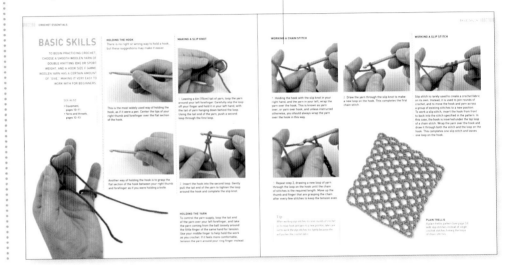

TECHNIQUES AND STITCHES

From the easiest of striped patterns to the lacy delights of filet crochet, the Techniques and Stitches chapter demonstrates a wide range of crochet stitches and techniques. Beginning with simple patterns and shapes, it moves on to textured stitches and non-standard techniques such as hairpin and Tunisian crochet, and finally explains how to make embellishments like cords and fringes, and how to add beads and sequins. The accompanying Stitch Collections show how to put the techniques into practice.

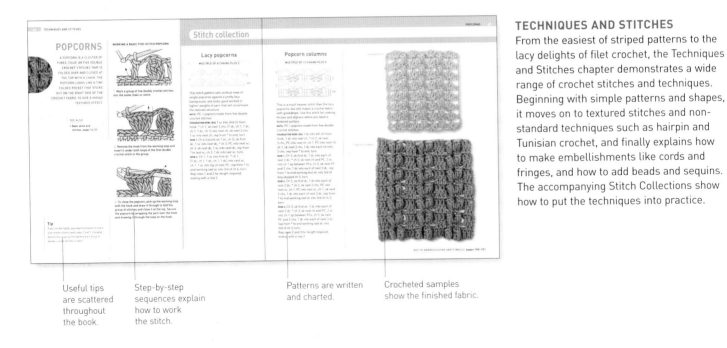

Useful tips are scattered throughout the book.

Step-by-step sequences explain how to work the stitch.

Patterns are written and charted.

Crocheted samples show the finished fabric.

Clear instructions list materials, finished size, gauge, and how to make up the item.

Each project is illustrated with an inspirational picture of the finished item.

PROJECTS

This chapter features seven attractive projects, ranging from a simple scarf worked in a pretty lace stitch to a gorgeous striped bag crocheted entirely in the round using a selection of contrasting yarns. All of the projects encourage you to use and expand on the techniques you have learned in the previous chapter.

GALLERY

This chapter showcases some of the different ways of using crochet fabric, from making stylish garments to creating home accessories. Crochet fabric is a textile with a huge range of possibilities—it can be light, delicate, and lacy, chunky and textured, or smooth and patterned in a variety of ways. Organized into categories such as garments and bags, you can dip into the gallery anywhere for instant inspiration.

Each item is described with useful information on how it was created.

Vibrant color pictures provide inspiration and ideas for color schemes, stitches, and possibilities for your own projects.

SWATCH SIZES

Unless indicated otherwise, all of the crochet samples in this book were made using double knitting yarn and are shown in proportion to each other (approximately 80–85% actual size). This will help you to compare the sizes, textures, and overall effect of the different stitch patterns in relation to each other.

CHAPTER ONE

Crochet Essentials

This chapter contains all the key skills you need to get started with crochet. From choosing yarn and hooks to working the basic stitches and understanding both written and charted crochet patterns, this is the place to start, whether you are a beginner or someone who wants to freshen up existing crochet skills.

EQUIPMENT

TO TAKE UP CROCHET, ALL YOU NEED IS A CROCHET HOOK AND A BALL OF YARN. HOOKS ARE AVAILABLE IN A WIDE RANGE OF SIZES AND MATERIALS. AS YOU PROGRESS IN THE CRAFT, YOU CAN COLLECT MORE EQUIPMENT AS YOU NEED IT.

HOOKS

Hooks from different manufacturers, and those made from different materials, can vary widely in shape and size, even though they may all be branded with the same number or letter to indicate their size. Although the hook sizes quoted in pattern instructions are a very useful guide, you may find that you need to use smaller or larger hook sizes, depending on the brand, to achieve the correct gauge for a pattern. The most important thing to consider when choosing a hook is how it feels in your hand, and the ease with which it works with your yarn.

When you have discovered your perfect brand of hook, it is useful to buy a range of several different sizes so that they are always available to you. Store your hooks in a clean container such as a cosmetic bag. If the hook you are using starts to feel greasy or sticky, wash it in warm water with a little detergent, rinse with clean water, and dry thoroughly.

COMMON HOOKS

The most common types of hooks are made from aluminum or plastic, and they come in a wide range of sizes to suit different yarn weights. Handmade wooden and horn hooks are also available, many featuring decorative handles.

SMALL HOOKS

Small sizes of steel hooks are made for working crochet with fine cotton yarns (this type of fine work is sometimes called thread crochet). These hooks often have plastic handles to give a better grip.

DOUBLE-ENDED HOOKS

These have a different size of hook at each end. This example has a thumb plate in the middle, but many double-ended hooks have a straight shaft and can be used for adapted Tunisian crochet patterns.

SPECIALIZED HOOKS

Specialist hooks with easy-to-hold handles are useful additions to a hook collection.

USEFUL YARN/HOOK COMBINATIONS
Refer to page 152 for recommended hook sizes to use with different weights of yarn to achieve commonly used gauge ranges.

LARGE KNITTING NEEDLES OR BROOMSTICK PINS
Plastic needles are easier to maneuver when working broomstick crochet.

STITCH MARKERS
These can be looped through stitches to mark a particular point in a pattern.

TAPE MEASURE
Look for measures with both inches and centimeters marked along their length.

LARGE-HEADED PINS
Use these for securing fabric before seaming and for marking stitches.

SCISSORS
Small, sharp scissors are the most useful.

NEEDLE CASE
Use this to protect yarn needles and keep them safe.

YARN NEEDLES
These have blunt points and long eyes. Bent-tip and tapestry needles are both useful for seaming.

FLEXIBLE TUNISIAN CROCHET HOOKS
These are perfect for making large shawls and afghans worked in Tunisian crochet.

TUNISIAN CROCHET HOOKS
These look like knitting needles with a hook at one end.

YARNS AND THREADS

YARNS COME IN A WIDE VARIETY OF MATERIALS, WEIGHTS, COLORS, AND PRICE RANGES.

There is a huge range of yarns available to use for crochet, from very fine cotton to bulky wool. Yarns can be made from one fiber or combine a mixture of two or three different fibers in varying proportions.

NATURAL FIBERS
Woolen yarns and blended yarns with a high proportion of wool feel good to crochet with because they have a certain amount of stretch. Silk yarn has a delightful luster, but it is less resilient than either wool or cotton and is more expensive. Yarns made from cotton and linen are durable and cool to wear, but may be blended with other fibers to add softness.

HANDSPUN YARN
Look for fibers you like working with and that have a tight, smooth twist if you require good stitch definition.

WOOL
Produces a light, stretchy fabric with good drape. [Sample made with size F (4mm) hook.]

ALPACA
Produces a firm fabric with good stitch definition, but with more warmth and loft than cotton. [Sample made with size F (4mm) hook.]

MERCERIZED COTTON
Produces a firm fabric with good stitch definition. [Sample made with size F (4mm) hook.]

SILK
Good stitch definition and drape.

LINEN
Crisp, with good stitch definition; the fabric softens with washing and wear. [Sample made with size F (4mm) hook.]

TWEED WOOL BLEND
Light and stretchy, the fabric improves with age, but a strong tweed effect can dull the stitch definition. [Sample made with size F (4mm) hook.]

SYNTHETIC YARNS

Yarns made wholly from synthetic fibers, such as acrylic or nylon, are usually less expensive to buy than those made from natural fibers, but can pill when worn and lose their shape. A good solution is to choose a yarn with a small proportion of synthetic fibers combined with a natural fiber, such as wool or cotton.

Self striping cotton

Fine crochet cotton

Crochet cotton with lurex

Silk rolls

Rayon

Fine crochet cotton

KID MOHAIR

The twist and treatment of mohair can make it more or less fluffy.

KID MOHAIR/SILK BLEND

Produces a fine, open fabric with good drape and texture. [Sample made with size F (4mm) hook. A smaller hook would produce better stitch definition, but the nature of the yarn would be lost.]

FINE CROCHET COTTONS AND THREADS

A variety of fibers can be spun into threads and used for crochet. The nature of the fabric is dictated by the fiber content, but it is also influenced by hook size. Rolls of silk thread are perfect for tiny edgings and flowers. Shiny rayons are strong and durable. Cotton and lurex blends are available if you want glitter. [Sample made with size 7 (1.5mm) steel hook.]

SILK RIBBON YARN

Produces a bulky, open fabric with good drape and texture. [Sample made with size K (6.5mm) hook.]

SOCK YARN

The addition of some nylon to the wool or cotton strengthens the fabric but has little effect on the stitches. [Sample made with size C/D (3mm) hook.]

SILK AND BEADS

This yarn has been spun with a length of beaded thread. The random beading would be more visible on an open mesh fabric. [Sample made with size H (5mm) hook.]

UNUSUAL YARN COMBINATIONS

Spinners strive to intrigue and seduce crocheters with unusual yarns, and the only clues are the fiber content and the twist — sometimes only a swatch will reveal a yarn's true beauty.

BASIC SKILLS

TO BEGIN PRACTICING CROCHET, CHOOSE A SMOOTH WOOLEN YARN OF DOUBLE KNITTING (DK) OR SPORT WEIGHT, AND A HOOK SIZE F (4MM). WOOLEN YARN HAS A CERTAIN AMOUNT OF "GIVE," MAKING IT VERY EASY TO WORK WITH FOR BEGINNERS.

SEE ALSO

- Equipment, pages 10–11
- Yarns and threads, pages 12–13

HOLDING THE HOOK

There is no right or wrong way to hold a hook, but these suggestions may make it easier.

This is the most widely used way of holding the hook, as if it were a pen. Center the tips of your right thumb and forefinger over the flat section of the hook.

Another way of holding the hook is to grasp the flat section of the hook between your right thumb and forefinger as if you were holding a knife.

MAKING A SLIP KNOT

1 Leaving a 6in (15cm) tail of yarn, loop the yarn around your left forefinger. Carefully slip the loop off your finger and hold it in your left hand, with the tail of yarn hanging down behind the loop. Using the tail end of the yarn, push a second loop through the first loop.

2 Insert the hook into the second loop. Gently pull the tail end of the yarn to tighten the loop around the hook and complete the slip knot.

HOLDING THE YARN

To control the yarn supply, loop the tail end of the yarn over your left forefinger, and take the yarn coming from the ball loosely around the little finger of the same hand for tension. Use your middle finger to help hold the work as you crochet. If it feels more comfortable, tension the yarn around your ring finger instead.

WORKING A CHAIN STITCH

1 Holding the hook with the slip knot in your right hand, and the yarn in your left, wrap the yarn over the hook. This is known as yarn over, or yarn over hook, and unless instructed otherwise, you should always wrap the yarn over the hook in this way.

2 Draw the yarn through the slip knot to make a new loop on the hook. This completes the first chain stitch.

3 Repeat step 2, drawing a new loop of yarn through the loop on the hook until the chain of stitches is the required length. Move up the thumb and finger that are grasping the chain after every few stitches to keep the tension even.

Tip

When working slip stitches to close rounds of crochet, or to move hook and yarn to a new position, take care not to work the slip stitches too tightly because this will pucker the crochet fabric.

WORKING A SLIP STITCH

Slip stitch is rarely used to create a crochet fabric on its own. Instead, it is used to join rounds of crochet, and to move the hook and yarn across a group of existing stitches to a new position. To work a slip stitch, insert the hook from front to back into the stitch specified in the pattern. In this case, the hook is inserted under the top loop of a chain stitch. Wrap the yarn over the hook and draw it through both the stitch and the loop on the hook. This completes one slip stitch and leaves one loop on the hook.

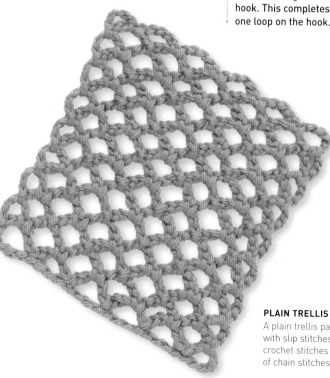

PLAIN TRELLIS
A plain trellis pattern (see page 53) with slip stitches instead of single crochet stitches linking the loops of chain stitches.

FOUNDATION CHAINS

THE FOUNDATION CHAIN IS THE CROCHET EQUIVALENT OF CASTING ON IN KNITTING. IT IS THE FOUNDATION FROM WHICH YOUR CROCHET FABRIC GROWS.

SEE ALSO

• Basic skills, pages 14–15

It is important to make sure that you have made the required number of chain stitches for the pattern you are going to work. The front of the foundation chain looks like a series of V-shapes or little hearts, while the back of the chain forms a distinctive "bump" of yarn behind each V-shape. Count the stitches on either the front or back of the chain, whichever you find easier.

COUNTING CHAINS

Count each V-shaped loop on the front of the chain as one chain stitch, except for the loop on the hook, which should not be counted. Alternatively, you may find it easier to turn the chain over and count the stitches on the back of the chain.

Back of chain

Front of chain

Not counted

LONG FOUNDATION CHAINS
Use stitch markers to help when counting a long foundation chain, slipping a marker into the chain to mark every 20 or so stitches.

WORKING INTO THE FOUNDATION CHAIN

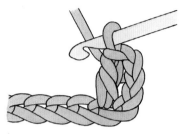

1 The first row of stitches is worked into the foundation chain. The hook can be inserted into the chain in different ways, but the method described here is the easiest one for a beginner, although it does give the crochet a rather loose edge. Holding the chain with the front facing you, insert the hook from front to back under the top loop of the appropriate chain stitch and work the first stitch as specified in the pattern.

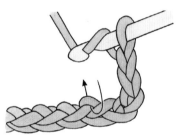

2 To make a stronger, neater edge that can stand alone without an edge finish being needed, turn the chain so that the back of it is facing you. Work the first row of stitches as instructed in the pattern, inserting the hook through the "bump" at the back of each chain stitch.

Tip
When working a foundation chain, most crocheters prefer to use a hook that is one size larger than the size used for the main crochet. This makes it easier to insert the hook when working the next row and stops the edge of the crochet from being too tight.

TURNING AND STARTING CHAINS

WHEN WORKING CROCHET IN ROWS OR ROUNDS, YOU WILL NEED TO WORK A SPECIFIC NUMBER OF EXTRA CHAIN STITCHES BEFORE BEGINNING EACH NEW ROW OR ROUND. THE EXTRA CHAINS ARE NEEDED TO BRING THE HOOK UP TO THE CORRECT HEIGHT FOR THE PARTICULAR CROCHET STITCH YOU WILL BE WORKING NEXT.

SEE ALSO

• Basic skills,
  pages 14–15

When the work is turned in order to begin a new row, the extra chains are called a turning chain. When the extra chains are worked at the beginning of a new round, they are called a starting chain. The illustration below shows the correct number of chain stitches needed to make a turn for each type of crochet stitch. If you tend to work chain stitches very tightly, you may need to work an extra chain in order to stop the edges of your work from becoming too tight. If you tend to work your chains loosely, then you may decide to work one less chain than specified in the pattern.

Single crochet stitch	1 turning chain
Half double crochet stitch	2 turning chains
Double crochet stitch	3 turning chains
Treble crochet stitch	4 turning chains

The turning or starting chain is usually counted as the first stitch of the row. For example, ch 4 (counts as 1 tr) at the beginning of a row or round means that the turning or starting chain contains four chain stitches, and these are counted as the equivalent of one treble crochet stitch. The exception is single crochet, when the single turning chain is ignored rather than being counted as a stitch. A turning or starting chain may be longer than the number required for the stitch, and in that case counts as one stitch plus a number of chains. For example, ch 6 (counts as 1 tr, ch 2) means that the turning or starting chain is the equivalent of one treble crochet stitch plus two chains.

At the end of the row or round, the final stitch is usually worked into the turning or starting chain of the previous row or round. The final stitch may be worked into the top chain stitch of the turning or starting chain, or into another specified stitch of the chain. For example, 1 dc into 3rd of ch 3 means that the final stitch is a double crochet stitch and should be worked into the 3rd stitch of the turning or starting chain.

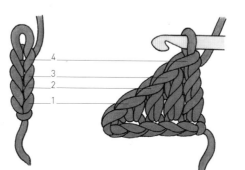

4
3
2
1

FILET CROCHET
The turning chain for this filet crochet design will include the chain that spans the first space.

SINGLE CROCHET STITCH

ONLY A SLIP STITCH OR CHAIN STITCH IS SHORTER THAN THE SINGLE CROCHET STITCH. SINGLE CROCHET CREATES A TIGHT, DENSE FABRIC.

SEE ALSO

• Foundation and turning chains, pages 16–17

1 Work the foundation chain, then insert the hook from front to back under the top loop of the second chain from the hook. Wrap the yarn over the hook and draw it through the chain, leaving two loops on the hook.

2 To complete the stitch, wrap the yarn over the hook and draw it through both loops on the hook. Continue in this way along the row, working one single crochet stitch into each chain.

3 At the end of the row, work one chain for the turning chain and turn (remember that this turning chain does not count as a stitch).

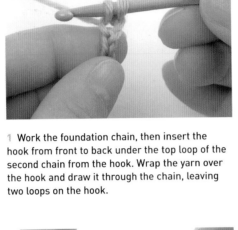

4 Insert the hook from front to back under both loops of the first single crochet stitch at the beginning of the row and work a single crochet stitch. Continue in this way, working a single crochet stitch into each remaining stitch made on the previous row. At the end of the row, work the final single crochet into the last stitch of the row below, not into the turning chain.

HALF DOUBLE CROCHET STITCH

SLIGHTLY TALLER THAN THE SINGLE CROCHET STITCH, THE HALF DOUBLE CROCHET STITCH CREATES A FABRIC WITH A SOFT, DENSE TEXTURE.

SEE ALSO

• Foundation and turning chains, pages 16–17

1 Work the foundation chain, then wrap the yarn over the hook and insert the hook from front to back under the top loop of the third chain from the hook.

2 Draw the yarn through the chain, leaving three loops on the hook.

3 Wrap the yarn over the hook and draw it through all three loops on the hook. This completes one half double crochet stitch and leaves one loop on the hook.

4 Continue in this way along the row, working one half double crochet stitch into each chain. At the end of the row, work two chains for the turning chain and turn.

5 Skipping the first half double crochet stitch at the beginning of the row, wrap the yarn over the hook, insert the hook from front to back under both loops of the second half double crochet stitch on the previous row, and work a half double crochet stitch. Continue in this way, working a half double crochet stitch into each remaining stitch made on the previous row. At the end of the row, work the last stitch into the top stitch of the turning chain.

DOUBLE CROCHET STITCH

DOUBLE CROCHET IS A POPULAR STITCH THAT IS OFTEN USED IN FILET CROCHET AS WELL AS IN MANY OTHER CROCHET FABRICS.

SEE ALSO
....
• Foundation and turning chains, pages 16–17

1 Work the foundation chain, then wrap the yarn over the hook and insert the hook from front to back under the top loop of the fourth chain from the hook. Draw the yarn through the chain, leaving three loops on the hook.

2 Wrap the yarn over the hook again and draw it through the first two loops on the hook, leaving two loops on the hook.

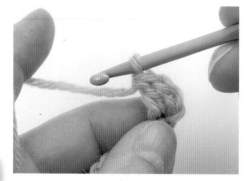

3 Wrap the yarn over the hook once more and draw it through the two loops on the hook. This completes one double crochet stitch and leaves one loop on the hook.

4 Continue in this way along the row, working one double crochet stitch into each chain. At the end of the row, work three chains for the turning chain and turn.

5 Skipping the first double crochet stitch at the beginning of the row, wrap the yarn over the hook, insert the hook from front to back under both loops of the second double crochet stitch on the previous row, and work a double crochet stitch. Continue in this way, working a double crochet stitch into each remaining stitch made on the previous row. At the end of the row, work the last stitch into the top stitch of the turning chain.

TREBLE CROCHET STITCH

TREBLE CROCHET IS A TALL STITCH WITH A LOOSE TEXTURE. IT IS RARELY WORKED ON ITS OWN IN COMPLETE ROWS TO PRODUCE A FABRIC.

SEE ALSO

• Foundation and turning chains, pages 16–17

1 Work the foundation chain, then wrap the yarn over the hook twice and insert the hook from front to back under the top loop of the fifth chain from the hook. Wrap the yarn over the hook again and draw the yarn through the chain, leaving four loops on the hook.

2 Wrap the yarn over the hook again and draw it through the first two loops on the hook (leaving three loops on the hook). Wrap the yarn over the hook again and draw it through the first two loops on the hook (leaving two loops on the hook).

3 Wrap the yarn over the hook once more and draw it through the remaining two loops on the hook. This completes one treble crochet stitch and leaves one loop on the hook.

4 At the end of the row, work four chains for the turning chain and turn. Wrap the yarn twice over the hook and insert the hook from front to back under both loops of the second stitch on the previous row, and work a treble crochet stitch as before. At the end of the row, work the last treble crochet stitch into the top stitch of the turning chain.

MEASURING GAUGE

THE TERM "GAUGE" REFERS TO THE NUMBER OF STITCHES AND ROWS CONTAINED IN A GIVEN WIDTH AND LENGTH OF CROCHET FABRIC. CROCHET PATTERNS INCLUDE A RECOMMENDED GAUGE FOR THE YARN THAT HAS BEEN USED TO MAKE THE ITEM SHOWN. IT IS IMPORTANT THAT YOU MATCH THIS GAUGE EXACTLY SO THAT YOUR WORK COMES OUT THE RIGHT SIZE.

SEE ALSO

- Pressing and blocking, pages 28–29

Gauge measurements are usually quoted as a specified number of stitches and rows to 4in (10cm) measured over a certain stitch pattern using a certain size of hook. The information may also include a measurement taken across one or more pattern repeats. Working to the suggested gauge will ensure that the crochet fabric is neither too heavy and stiff, nor too loose and floppy. Yarn ball bands or tags may also quote a recommended gauge as well as provide information on the yarn's fiber composition, yardage, and aftercare. Always try to use the exact yarn quoted in the pattern instructions. Two yarns of the same weight and fiber content made by different manufacturers will vary slightly in thickness.

Gauge can be affected by the type of yarn used, the size and brand of the crochet hook, the type of stitch pattern, and the gauge of an individual crocheter. No two people will crochet to exactly the same gauge, even when working with the identical hook and yarn. How you hold the hook, and the rate at which the yarn flows through your fingers, will affect the gauge you produce. Crochet fabric has less "give" and elasticity than a comparable knitted fabric, so it is crucial to make and measure a gauge swatch before you begin making any item. Accessories (purses, hats) and items of home furnishings (pillow covers, lace edgings) are often worked to a tighter gauge than scarves, garments, and afghans, which need a softer type of fabric with better drape.

MAKING AND MEASURING A GAUGE SAMPLE

Refer to the pattern instructions to find the recommended gauge. Working with the yarn and hook you will use for the item, make a generously sized sample 6–8in (15–20cm) wide. If you are working a stitch pattern, choose a number of foundation chains to suit the stitch repeat. Work in the required pattern until the piece is 6–8in (15–20cm) long. Fasten off the yarn. Block the gauge sample using the method suited to the yarn composition and allow to dry.

1 Lay the sample right side uppermost on a flat surface and use a ruler or tape measure to measure 4in (10cm) horizontally across a row of stitches. Mark this measurement by inserting two pins exactly 4in (10cm) apart. Make a note of the number of stitches (including partial stitches) between the pins. This is the number of stitches to 4in (10cm).

Recommended gauge

ZEN-COL-2

COLOR

DYE LOT

4", 10 cm
23 Rows
19 Stitches
4.75 sts = 1"

#9 (US)
5.5 mm

1.75oz • 50g
110yds • 100m

55% Cotton • Coton
45% Nylon • Nylon

Purchase sufficient yarn of this dye lot because the next lot may differ slightly in shade.

BERROCO

Zen Colors

First in fashion: www.berroco.com

BALL BANDS

Most yarn ball bands or tags carry information on recommended gauge. However, this is only a guide. Project information and your own judgment are more important.

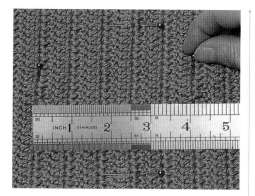

2 Turn the sample on its side. Working in the same way, measure 4in (10cm) across the rows, again inserting two pins exactly 4in (10cm) apart. Make a note of the number of rows (including partial rows) between the pins. This is the number of rows to 4in (10cm).

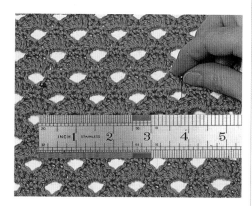

When working a particular stitch pattern, gauge information may be quoted as a multiple of the pattern repeat, rather than as a set number of rows and stitches. Work your gauge sample in pattern, but this time count repeats instead of rows and stitches between the pins.

HOW TO ADJUST THE GAUGE

If you have more stitches or pattern repeats between the pins inserted in your gauge sample, your gauge is too tight and you should make another sample using a hook one size larger. If you have fewer stitches or pattern repeats between the pins inserted in your gauge sample, your gauge is too loose and you should make another sample using a hook one size smaller. Block the new sample and measure the gauge as before. Repeat this process until your gauge matches that given in the pattern.

COMPARING GAUGE

Each of the three swatches on the right has 20 stitches and nine rows of double crochet worked in the same weight of yarn but using different sizes of hook. As well as altering the size of the swatch, the hook also affects the drape and handle of the crochet. Swatch 1 feels hard and stiff, while swatch 3 feels loose and floppy. Swatch 2 feels substantial but still has good drape.

Tip

The gauge may vary slightly as you work on a project. On some days you may be tense and work more tightly, while on other days your attention may wander and your gauge slacken. Check your gauge periodically as you work.

SWATCH 1
Double knitting yarn worked with a size C/D (3mm) hook.

SWATCH 2
Double knitting yarn worked with a size F (4mm) hook.

SWATCH 2
Double knitting yarn worked with a size J (5.5mm) hook.

JOINING, FASTENING OFF, AND WEAVING IN YARNS

THERE ARE A NUMBER OF METHODS YOU CAN USE TO JOIN A NEW BALL OF YARN INTO YOUR CROCHET. THE METHOD YOU CHOOSE CAN DEPEND ON WHETHER YOU ARE CONTINUING IN THE SAME COLOR OR INTRODUCING A NEW ONE.

JOINING YARN

When working in one color, try to join in a new ball of yarn at the end of the row rather than in the middle to make the join less noticeable. You can do this at the end of the row you are working by making an incomplete stitch and then using the new yarn to finish the stitch. Alternatively, join the new yarn at the beginning of the row you are about to work using the slip stitch method. When working color patterns, join the new color of yarn wherever the pattern or chart indicates by leaving the last stitch in the old color incomplete and using the new color to finish the stitch.

JOINING A NEW YARN IN SINGLE CROCHET

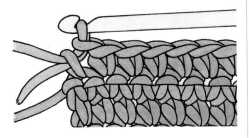

1 Join the new color at the end of the last row worked in the previous color. To work the last stitch, draw a loop of the old yarn through so that there are two loops on the hook. Loop the new yarn around the hook, then pull it through both loops on the hook. Turn and work the next row with the new color.

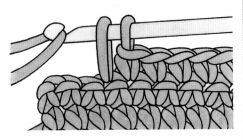

2 When working color patterns, join the new yarn color where the pattern or chart indicates. Leave the last stitch worked in the old color incomplete and proceed as above.

JOINING A NEW YARN USING SLIP STITCH

This method can be used when working any stitch. At the beginning of the row, make a slip knot in the new yarn and place it on the hook. Insert the hook into the first stitch of the row and make a slip stitch with the new yarn through both stitch and slip knot. Continue along the row using the new yarn.

JOINING A NEW YARN IN DOUBLE CROCHET

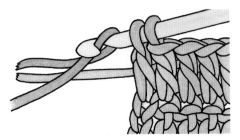

1 Join the new color at the end of the last row worked in the previous color. Leaving the last stage of the final stitch incomplete, loop the new yarn around the hook and pull it though the loops on the hook to complete the stitch.

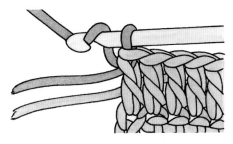

2 Turn and work the next row with the new color. You may find it easier to knot the two loose ends together before you cut the yarn no longer in use, leaving an end of about 4in (10cm). Always undo the knot before weaving in the yarn ends.

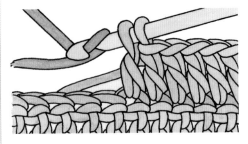

3 When working color patterns, join the new yarn color where the pattern or chart indicates. Leave the last stitch worked in the old color incomplete and proceed as above.

FASTENING OFF AND WEAVING IN YARN

It is very easy to fasten off yarn when you have finished a piece of crochet, but do not to cut the yarn too close to the work because you will need enough yarn to weave in the yarn end.

FASTENING OFF YARN

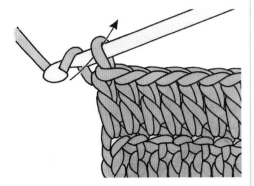

1 Cut the yarn about 6in (15cm) from the last stitch. Wrap the yarn over the hook and draw the yarn end through the loop on the hook.

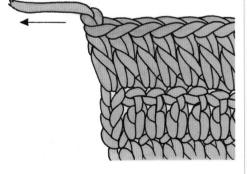

2 Gently pull the yarn to tighten the last stitch, then weave in the yarn end on the wrong side of the work.

It is important to fasten off and weave in yarn ends securely so that they do not unravel in wear or during laundering. Try to do this as neatly as possible, so that the woven yarn does not show through on the front of the work.

WEAVING IN A YARN END AT THE TOP EDGE

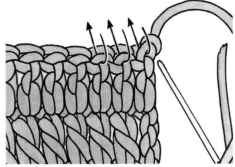

To weave in a yarn end along the top edge of a piece of crochet, start by threading the end into a yarn or tapestry needle. Take the needle through several stitches on the wrong side of the crochet, working stitch by stitch. Trim the remaining yarn.

WEAVING IN A YARN END AT THE LOWER EDGE

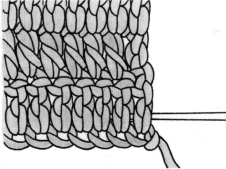

To weave in a yarn end along the lower edge of a piece of crochet, start by threading the end into a yarn or tapestry needle. Take the needle through several stitches on the wrong side of the crochet, then trim the remaining yarn.

WEAVING IN YARN ENDS ON A STRIPE PATTERN

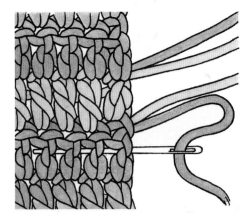

When weaving in yarn ends on a stripe pattern, or when using more than one yarn color, it pays to take a little more care in order to avoid the colors showing through on the right side of the fabric. Undo the knot securing the two yarn ends, thread the yarn or tapestry needle with one color, and weave in the end on the wrong side of the same color of stripe. Repeat with the second color.

DECORATIVE FEATURE

Yarns ends can become part of the design.

READING PATTERNS AND CHARTS

CROCHET PATTERNS COME IN DIFFERENT FORMS. THERE IS THE WRITTEN TYPE WHERE YOU MUST FOLLOW THE WRITTEN INSTRUCTIONS LINE BY LINE. THE SAME INSTRUCTIONS CAN ALSO BE SHOWN AS A SYMBOL CHART, WHICH MAY ACCOMPANY WRITTEN INSTRUCTIONS OR REPLACE THEM ENTIRELY. A FILET CROCHET DESIGN IS USUALLY SHOWN AS A BLACK-AND-WHITE CHART GIVING THE POSITION OF THE BLOCKS AND SPACES THAT MAKE UP THE DESIGN. JACQUARD AND INTARSIA PATTERNS HAVE THEIR OWN TYPE OF CHARTS WHERE EACH STITCH IS REPRESENTED BY A BLOCK OF COLOR, IN THE SAME WAY AS A CHART FOR A CROSS-STITCH DESIGN.

SEE ALSO

• Filet crochet,
  pages 56–59
• Jacquard patterns,
  pages 68–69
• Intarsia patterns,
  pages 70–71
• Abbreviations and
  symbols, pages 150–151

WRITTEN INSTRUCTIONS

At first sight the terminology of crochet can look rather complicated. The most important thing to remember when following a pattern is to check that you start off with the correct number of stitches in the foundation chain or ring, and then work through the instructions exactly as stated.

In a written pattern, square brackets and asterisks are used to make the pattern shorter and to avoid tedious repetition. Instructions may be phrased slightly differently depending on whether square brackets or asterisks are used, and both may be used together in the same pattern row of a complex design. The sequence of stitches enclosed inside square brackets must be worked as instructed.

For example, [1 dc into each of next 2 sts, ch 2] 3 times means that you will work the two double crochet stitches and the two chains three times in all. The instruction may also be expressed like this: * 1 dc into each of next 2 sts, ch 2; rep from * twice. The information is exactly the same, but it is stated in a slightly different way.

You may also find asterisks used in instructions. These tell you how to work any stitches remaining after the last complete repeat of a stitch sequence is worked. For example, rep from * to end, ending with 1 dc into each of last 2 sts, turn, means that you have two stitches left at the end of the row after working the last repeat. In this case, work one double crochet stitch into each of the last two stitches before turning to begin the next row.

You will also find round brackets in written instructions. They usually contain extra information, not instructions that have to be worked. For example, Row 1: (RS) means that the right side of the work is facing you as you work this row. Round brackets are also used to indicate the number of different sizes in which a garment pattern is worked, as well as the different numbers of stitches. In this case, it is helpful to read right through the pattern and highlight the corresponding numbers as an aid to easy reading. You may also find a number enclosed in round brackets at the end of a row

WRITTEN PATTERNS

Written patterns use abbreviations to save space and avoid repetition.

FOUNDATION RING: Ch 6 and join with sl st to form a ring.
ROUND 1: Ch 3 (counts as 1 dc), 15 dc into ring, join with sl st into 3rd of ch 3. (16 dc)
ROUND 2: Ch 5 (counts as 1 dc, ch 2), [1 dc into next dc, ch 2] 15 times, join with sl st into 3rd of ch 5. — Round brackets
ROUND 3: Ch 3, 2 dc into ch 2 sp, ch 1, [3 dc, ch 1] into each ch 2 sp to end, join with sl st into 3rd of ch 3. — Square brackets
ROUND 4: * [Ch 3, 1 sc into next ch 1 sp] 3 times, ch 6 (corner sp made), 1 sc into next ch 1 sp; rep from * — Asterisks to end, join with sl st into first of ch 3.

or round—this indicates the total number of stitches you have worked in that particular row or round. For example, (12 dc) at the end of a round means that you have worked 12 double crochet stitches in the round.

Each crochet stitch pattern worked in rows is written using a specific number of pattern rows and the sequence is repeated until the piece of crochet is the correct length. When working a complicated pattern, always make a note of exactly which row you are working because it is very easy to forget this if your crochet session gets interrupted.

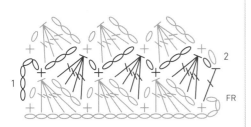

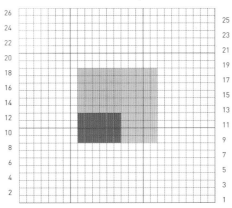

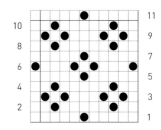

SYMBOL CHARTS

Some crochet patterns use symbol charts to describe the method of working visually. Symbols indicate the different stitches and where and how they should be placed in relation to one another. A symbol chart will still contain some written instructions, but the stitch patterns are shown in a visual form and not written out line by line. Each row will either be shown in a color that echoes the color used for the swatch, or alternate rows will be in tints of the color so that it is easier to follow progress along the row.

To use a symbol chart, first familiarize yourself with the different symbols. There is a key to the symbols used in the charts on pages 150–151. Each symbol represents a single instruction or stitch and indicates where to work the stitch. Follow the numerical sequence on the chart whether you are working in rows or rounds.

COLOR BLOCK CHARTS

Jacquard and intarsia patterns are shown as a colored chart on a grid. Each colored square on the chart represents one stitch and you should always work upward from the bottom of the chart, reading odd-numbered rows (right side rows) from right to left and even-numbered rows (wrong side rows) from left to right.

Begin by working the foundation chain in the first color, then work the pattern from the chart, starting at the bottom right-hand corner and joining in new colors as they occur in the design. On the first row, work the first stitch into the second chain from the hook, then work the rest of the row in single crochet.

FILET CROCHET CHARTS

Filet crochet charts are numbered at the sides and you should follow the numbered sequence upward from the bottom of the chart, working from side to side. Each open square on the chart represents one space and each solid square represents a block.

Tiny flowers pattern (see page 59) worked from a filet crochet chart.

Intarsia block (see page 71) worked from a color block chart.

Angled clusters pattern (see page 40) worked from a symbol chart.

PRESSING AND BLOCKING

A LIGHT PRESS ON THE WRONG SIDE WITH A COOL IRON IS OFTEN ALL THE TREATMENT THAT PIECES OF CROCHET NEED BEFORE BEING STITCHED TOGETHER, BUT SOME PIECES, SUCH AS GARMENT SECTIONS AND CROCHETED MOTIFS, WILL NEED MORE ATTENTION.

BLOCKING A GARMENT AFTER ASSEMBLY

You can block a garment after assembly by immersing the crochet in cool water for a few minutes so that the water penetrates all of the yarn fibers. Do not lift the crochet out, but support it with your hand as you drain away the water. The aim is to avoid stretching the work. Gently squeeze out the excess water but do not wring. Roll the crochet in a towel to blot away excess moisture. Lay the crochet flat on a clean towel and pat it into shape. Leave it in a warm place, away from direct sunlight, to dry completely. This method is useful if you ever need to reshape a garment.

The process of blocking involves easing and pinning the crocheted pieces into the correct shape on a fabric-covered board, then either steaming with an iron or moistening with cold water, depending on the fiber content of the yarn. Always be guided by the information given on the ball band of the yarn because most synthetic fibers are easily damaged by heat. When in doubt, choose the cold water method for blocking synthetic fibers.

Yarns made from most natural fibers (cotton, linen, and wool, but not silk, which is more delicate) can be blocked with warm steam. A large item, such as a blanket or throw made in one piece (or from motifs that have been joined together as you go), can be carefully pressed on the wrong side over a well-padded ironing board, using a light touch to avoid crushing the stitches. Do not steam or hot press a crochet piece made from yarns containing synthetic fibers such as nylon or acrylic—you will flatten it and make the yarn limp and lifeless. Instead, use a cool iron or the cold water blocking method.

To block garment pieces and large quantities of separate motifs, it is a good idea to make a blocking board. You can do this inexpensively by covering a 24 x 36in (60 x 90cm) piece of flat

ROLLING IN A TOWEL

Shaped projects, such as hats and seamed items, may be blocked by soaking them in cold water and rolling them in a towel to remove the excess water. They can then be pulled and eased into shape and left to dry away from direct heat or sunlight. Hats may be placed over an upturned bowl or a hat stretcher to dry.

board (a lightweight pinboard made from cork is ideal) with one or two layers of quilter's batting. Secure the batting on the back of the board with staples or thumb tacks, then cover with a layer of fabric and secure in the same way. Choose fabric made from cotton so that it can withstand the heat of the iron. A checked pattern is useful so that the lines can help you when pinning out straight edges.

Use plenty of rustproof pins to pin out the pieces, and make sure that the pins have glass rather than plastic heads because plastic will melt when heat is applied. When pinning out long pieces of crochet, such as edgings, work in sections and allow each section to dry completely before moving on to the next section.

PINNING THE PIECES

Pin out the piece, inserting the pins through both the fabric and batting layers. Be generous with the amount of pins you use around the edges, and gently ease the crochet into shape before inserting each pin. Unless the piece is heavily textured and needs blocking face up, you can block crochet with either the right side or wrong side facing upward.

BLOCKING NATURAL FIBER YARNS

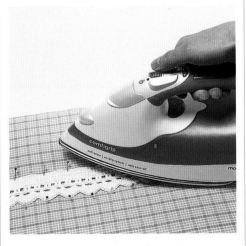

To block natural fiber yarns, pin out the pieces and hold a steam iron set at the correct temperature for the yarn about ¾in (2cm) above the surface of the crochet. Allow the steam to penetrate for several seconds. Work in sections and do not allow the iron to come into contact with the crochet surface. Lay the board flat and allow the crochet to dry before removing the pins.

BLOCKING SYNTHETIC FIBER YARNS

To block synthetic fiber yarns, pin out the pieces and use a spray bottle to mist the crochet with cold water until it is evenly moist all over, but not saturated. When blocking heavyweight yarns, gently pat the crochet with your hand to help the moisture penetrate more easily. Lay the board flat and allow the crochet to dry before removing the pins.

Tip

If you are planning to block lots of pieces of crochet of the same size, such as square motifs to make an afghan, it is a good idea to make a special blocking board so that you can pin out six or more pieces at a time. Use a pencil to mark the outlines of several squares of the correct dimensions on a piece of plain, light-colored fabric, allowing about 2in (5cm) of space between the squares for ease of pinning. Use the fabric to cover a blocking board as described opposite.

SEAMS

THERE ARE SEVERAL METHODS OF JOINING PIECES OF CROCHET BY SEWING OR USING A CROCHET HOOK. USE THE SAME YARN FOR BOTH CROCHET FABRIC AND SEAMS, UNLESS THE YARN IS THICK OR TEXTURED, IN WHICH CASE USE A FINER YARN OF MATCHING COLOR.

SEE ALSO
• Basic skills and stitches, pages 14–21

Tip
It is a good idea to try out some of the seams shown here before assembling a project. Crochet a couple of samples in your project stitch, then use contrasting yarn for seaming so that you can easily unpick the seam if you do not like the effect and wish to try a different method.

USING A YARN OR TAPESTRY NEEDLE

A back stitch or chain stitch seam is durable and good for joining irregular edges, but can be rather bulky, depending on the weight of the yarn. These methods are good for seaming loose-fitting garments such as winter sweaters and jackets. A woven seam gives a flatter finish because straight edges are joined edge to edge. Woven seams work best when making up fine work and baby garments.

BACK STITCH SEAM

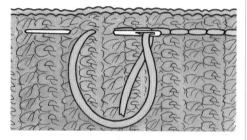

Place the pieces to be joined together with right sides facing and pin together, inserting the pins at right angles to the edge. Thread a yarn or tapestry needle with matching yarn and work a row of back stitches from right to left, one or two stitches away from the edge.

CHAIN STITCH SEAM

This is the stitched version of the slip stitch seam shown opposite. Place the pieces to be joined together with right sides facing and pin together, inserting the pins at right angles to the edge. Thread a yarn or tapestry needle with matching yarn and work a row of chain stitches from right to left, close to the edge.

WOVEN SEAM

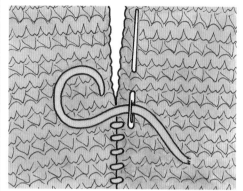

Place the pieces to be joined side by side on a flat surface with wrong sides facing upward and row ends touching. Thread a yarn or tapestry needle with matching yarn and work a vertical row of evenly spaced stitches in a loose zigzag from edge to edge, carefully tightening the tension of the stitches as you work so that the edges pull together. For a single crochet fabric, pick up one stitch; for double crochet, pick up half a stitch.

JOINING UPPER OR LOWER EDGES

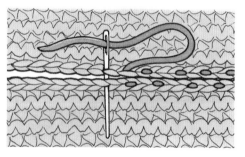

Place the pieces to be joined side by side on a flat surface with wrong sides facing upward and edges touching. Thread a yarn or tapestry needle with matching yarn and work a horizontal row of evenly spaced stitches, working from edge to edge and carefully tightening the tension of the stitches as you work so that the edges pull together.

USING A CROCHET HOOK

Single crochet seams are good for joining straight edges because they are less bulky than slip stitch seams. Single crochet seams can also be used on the right side of a garment—work the seams in contrasting yarn to make a decorative statement. Single crochet and chain seams, and alternating slip stitch seams, both give a flatter effect than single crochet seams, and have the advantage of being slightly stretchy.

SLIP STITCH SEAM

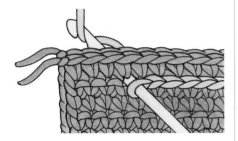

This is the crochet version of the chain stitch seam shown opposite. Place the pieces to be joined together with right sides facing and pin together, inserting the pins at right angles to the edge. Holding the yarn behind the work, insert the hook through both layers of fabric and draw a loop of yarn through both layers, leaving a loop on the hook. Repeat, working from right to left. Secure the yarn end carefully because slip stitch can unravel easily.

SINGLE CROCHET SEAM ALONG ROW EDGES

Place the pieces to be joined together with right sides facing for a concealed seam, or wrong sides facing for a decorative seam. Pin the layers together, inserting the pins at right angles to the edge. Holding the yarn behind the work, insert the hook through both layers of fabric and work a row of single crochet stitches close to the edge. Space the stitches so that the work remains flat without stretching or puckering.

SINGLE CROCHET SEAM ALONG UPPER OR LOWER EDGES

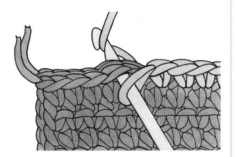

Place the pieces to be joined together with wrong sides facing and edges aligned. Pin the layers together, inserting the pins at right angles to the edge. Holding the yarn behind the work, insert the hook through corresponding stitches on both layers and work a row of single crochet stitches along the edge.

SINGLE CROCHET AND CHAIN SEAM

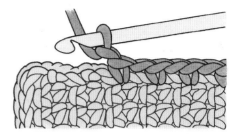

Place the pieces to be joined together with right sides facing and pin together, inserting the pins at right angles to the edge. Holding the yarn behind the work, insert the hook through both layers of fabric and work a single crochet stitch at the beginning of the seam. Work a chain, then work another single crochet stitch a short distance from the first. Repeat evenly along the edge, alternating single crochet stitches and chains, and ending with a single crochet stitch.

ALTERNATING SLIP STITCH SEAM

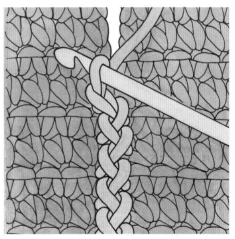

Place the pieces to be joined side by side on a flat surface with wrong sides facing upward and row ends touching. Work a slip stitch at the bottom corner of the right-hand piece, then work another in the corresponding stitch on the left-hand piece. Continue to work slip stitches along the seam, alternating from side to side.

CHAPTER TWO

Techniques and Stitches

This chapter takes you through a wide range of crochet techniques, from working in the round, colorwork, and filet crochet to making sew-on embellishments and edgings. Throughout the chapter you will find special stitch collections featuring swatches and instructions for a variety of openwork, lace, and textured stitch patterns.

STRIPE PATTERNS

WORKING STRIPES OF COLOR IS THE EASIEST WAY TO ADD PATTERN TO A PIECE OF CROCHET THAT IS WORKED IN ONE OF THE BASIC STITCHES. SIMPLE HORIZONTAL STRIPES WORKED IN TWO, THREE, OR MORE COLORS ADD ZING TO A PLAIN GARMENT OR ACCESSORY.

SEE ALSO
• Basic skills and stitches, pages 14–21
• Joining yarns, page 24

USING DIFFERENT YARN WEIGHTS
Calculate the gauge and the number of stitches for the row or round for each yarn weight and work two stitches into one stitch or crochet two stitches together as required.

Stripes can be strongly contrasting in color, worked in different shades of one color for a more subtle effect, or combine one basic color with one or more coordinating colors. Single crochet, half double crochet, and double crochet all look good worked in stripes.

Working magic stripes is a fun way of using up oddments of yarn that are left over from making other projects. You can use any short lengths of yarn, depending on the width of crochet fabric you are making, but magic stripes look best when the color changes at least once on every row. Choose yarns of similar weight and fiber composition when making garments, but for accessories and pillow covers you can combine different weights and textures.

REDUCING THE NUMBER OF YARN ENDS
Instead of breaking off each color of yarn when you change to another one, you can carry the colors not in use up the side of the work when working some stripe patterns. As well as being faster, this means that you have fewer yarn ends to deal with when you finish crocheting. You can do this when working a stripe pattern with an even number of rows using two colors, or an odd number of rows using three colors.

WORKING STRIPES WITHOUT BREAKING OFF YARN

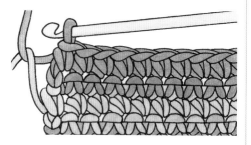

When working patterns of wide stripes that have an even number of rows, carry the color not in use up the side of the work, but twist the two yarns together every two rows to avoid making big loops at the edge.

CHANGING YARNS AT THE END OF A ROW
This method works with all crochet stitches.

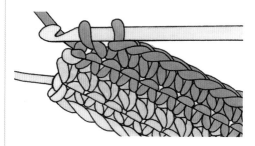

1 Work the foundation chain and the first two rows using the first color (yarn A). Join in the second color (yarn B) without breaking off yarn A. Work to the last stitch, leaving two loops of yarn B on the hook.

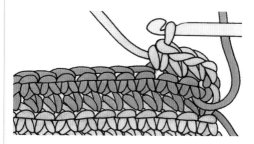

2 Drop yarn B and pick up yarn A at the side of the work. Complete the stitch with yarn A, turn, and work the next two rows using yarn A.

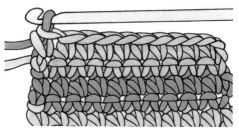

3 At the end of the second row in yarn A, drop yarn A and complete the final stitch with yarn B. Continue working with yarn B for two rows, then repeat the two-row stripes, alternating the yarn colors as required.

Stitch collection

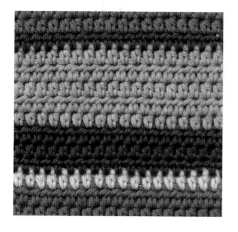

Random stripes

ANY NUMBER OF CH PLUS TURNING CH

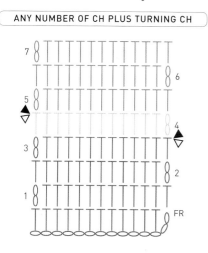

Worked in rows of half double crochet stitches, the stripes are of different widths and arranged in a random color sequence. Work several rows in yarn A, then continue working in the same stitch, changing colors randomly, after one, two, three, or more rows have been worked.

Repeating stripes

ANY NUMBER OF CH PLUS TURNING CH

Worked in rows of single crochet stitches, the stripes are of different widths and arranged in a repeating color sequence. Work two rows in yarn A, four in yarn B, four in yarn C, and two in yarn D, then repeat the color sequence from the beginning. This type of arrangement is also called a sequenced stripe pattern.

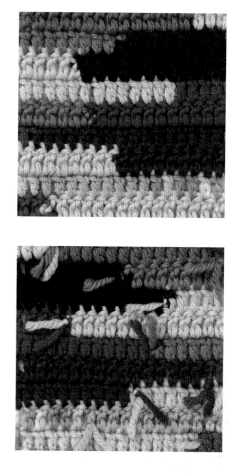

Magic stripes

ANY NUMBER OF CH PLUS TURNING CH

Begin by winding all the yarn lengths into balls and knotting the ends together about ¾in (2cm) from the end, mixing colors at random. Work in rows of double crochet stitches, pushing the knots through to the same side as you work. You can use either side of the crochet fabric as your right side.

RIDGE STITCHES

UNLESS A PATTERN INSTRUCTS OTHERWISE, IT IS USUAL TO WORK MOST CROCHET STITCHES BY TAKING THE HOOK UNDER BOTH LOOPS OF THE STITCHES MADE ON THE PREVIOUS ROW. BY WORKING UNDER JUST ONE LOOP, EITHER THE BACK OR THE FRONT LOOP OF A STITCH, THE UNWORKED LOOP BECOMES A HORIZONTAL RIDGE, AND THE CHARACTER AND APPEARANCE OF EVEN THE MOST BASIC CROCHET FABRIC CHANGES.

SEE ALSO
- Basic skills and stitches, pages 14–21

NEAT EDGES ON A RIDGE STITCH FABRIC
When working crochet stitches taller than single crochet into either the front or back loops of each stitch, you may find that the edges of the fabric become unstable and stretchy. To prevent this, try working into both loops of the first and last stitches on every row.

Ridge stitches are not used for decorative reasons but have practical uses. A row or round of ridge stitches will make the fabric easier to fold at this point, and so they are often used on flaps and collars. For small, fiddly shapes, rounds of stitches are often worked under the back loop only because it is easier to insert a hook under just one loop than under two. The ridges produced on double crochet are less pronounced than those on single crochet, but the drape and the elasticity of the fabric are greatly improved.

WORKING INTO THE FRONT LOOP OF SINGLE CROCHET

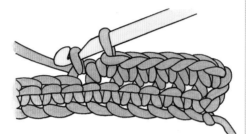

Insert the hook only under the front loop of the stitches on the previous row—the top loop nearest to you as you work the row.

WORKING INTO THE BACK LOOP OF SINGLE CROCHET

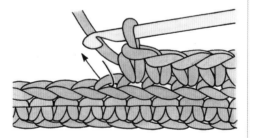

Insert the hook only under the back loop of the stitches on the previous row—the top loop farthest away from you as you work the row. Working into the back loops of a row of single crochet stitches creates a strongly ridged fabric.

WORKING INTO THE FRONT LOOP OF DOUBLE CROCHET

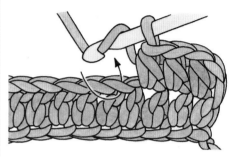

Work in the same way as for single crochet, but when you reach the end of the row, work under the back bump and front loop of the specified stitch of the turning chain.

WORKING INTO THE BACK LOOP OF DOUBLE CROCHET

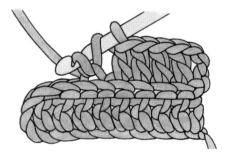

Work in the same way as for single crochet, but when you reach the end of the row, work under the back loop and back bump of the specified stitch of the turning chain.

Stitch collection

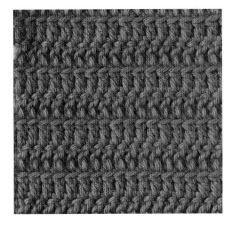

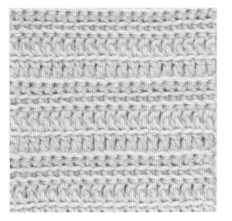

Wide ridges

> ANY NUMBER OF CHAINS PLUS 3

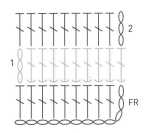

This stitch pattern has a ridged right side and smooth wrong side. The ridged side has fairly subtle ridges that are spaced widely apart.

FOUNDATION ROW: (RS) 1 dc into 4th ch from hook, 1 dc into each ch to end, turn.

ROW 1: Ch 3 (counts as 1 dc), 1 dc into front loop of each dc to end working last dc into 3rd of ch 3, turn.

ROW 2: Ch 3 (counts as 1 dc), 1 dc into both loops of each dc to end working last dc into 3rd of ch 3, turn.

Rep rows 1 and 2 for length required, ending with a row 1.

Faux ribbing

> ANY NUMBER OF CHAINS PLUS 1

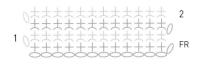

This stitch looks rather like knitted ribbing and both sides are identical. It can be worked in narrow bands to edge cuffs and hems on a crochet garment, or used as a textured pattern stitch in its own right.

FOUNDATION ROW: 1 sc into 2nd ch from hook, 1 sc into each ch to end, turn.

ROW 1: Ch 1, 1 sc into back loop of each sc to end, turn.

Rep row 1 for length required.

Simple ridges

> ANY NUMBER OF CHAINS PLUS 3

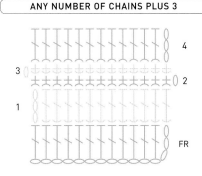

This stitch pattern has a ridged side and a smooth side.

FOUNDATION ROW: 1 dc into 4th ch from hook, 1 dc into each ch to end, turn.

ROW 1: Ch 3 (counts as 1 dc), 1 dc into front loop of each dc to end working last dc into 3rd of beg skipped ch 3, turn.

ROW 2: Ch 1, 1 sc into back loop of each dc to end working last sc into 3rd of ch 3, turn.

ROW 3: Ch 1, 1 sc into front loop of each sc to end, turn.

ROW 4: Ch 3 (counts as 1 dc), 1 dc into back loop of each sc to end, turn.

Rep rows 1–4 for length required, ending with a row 2.

KEY TO ABBREVIATIONS AND SYMBOLS pages 150–151

SHAPING

THERE ARE SEVERAL DIFFERENT
METHODS OF SHAPING YOUR
CROCHET GARMENTS BY
INCREASING AND DECREASING
THE NUMBER OF STITCHES.

SEE ALSO
• Basic skills and
  stitches, pages 14–21

MITERED BLOCK
Working an internal
decrease (sc3tog) at
the center of every row
creates a neat square
of single crochet.

MAKING A NEAT EDGE
To make a neat edge at the beginning of
a row, work the first stitch and then work
the increase. At the end of a row, work
until two stitches remain (the last stitch
will probably be the turning chain from
the previous row). Work the increase into
the penultimate stitch, then work the
last stitch as usual.

Adding or subtracting one or two stitches at
intervals along a row of crochet is the easiest
way of shaping. This process is known as
working internal increases or decreases.
When groups of stitches are added or
subtracted at the beginning and end of
specified rows, this is known as working
external increases or decreases. The methods
can be used with single, half double, double,
and treble crochet stitches.

WORKING A SINGLE INTERNAL INCREASE

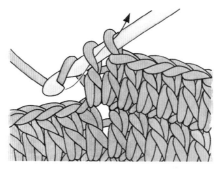

The simplest method of working a single increase
(adding a single stitch) at intervals along a row of
crochet is by working two stitches into one stitch
on the previous row.

WORKING A DOUBLE INTERNAL INCREASE

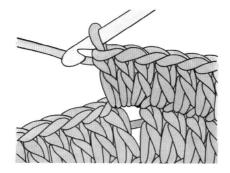

To work a double increase (adding two stitches)
at intervals along the row, work three stitches
into one stitch on the previous row.

WORKING AN INTERNAL DECREASE
IN SINGLE CROCHET

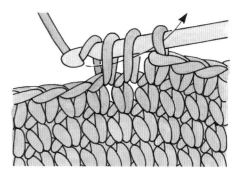

Decrease one single crochet stitch by working
two stitches together (sc2tog). Leave the first
stitch incomplete so that there are two loops
on the hook, then draw the yarn through the
next stitch so that you have three loops on
the hook. Yarn over and pull through all three
loops to finish the decrease. Two stitches can
be decreased in the same way by working
three stitches together (sc3tog).

WORKING AN INTERNAL DECREASE
IN DOUBLE CROCHET

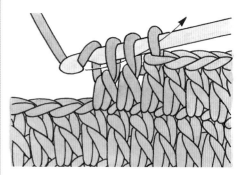

Decrease one double crochet stitch by working
two stitches together (dc2tog). Leave the first
stitch incomplete so that there are two loops on
the hook, then work another incomplete stitch
so that you have three loops on the hook. Yarn
over and pull through all three loops to finish
the decrease. Two stitches can be decreased in
the same way by working three double crochet
stitches together (dc3tog).

WORKING AN EXTERNAL INCREASE

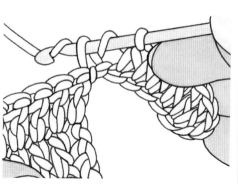

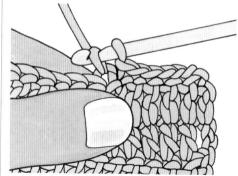

1 To increase several stitches at one time, you will need to add extra foundation chains at the appropriate end of the row. To add stitches at the beginning of a row, work the required number of extra chains at the end of the previous row. Do not forget to add the correct number of turning chains for the stitch you are using.

2 Turn and work back along the extra chains, then work along the rest of the row in the usual way. In this case, the stitches have been worked into one loop of the extra chains, but for easier seaming and a firmer edge, work into the bump on the reverse of the chains.

WORKING AN EXTERNAL DECREASE

To decrease several stitches at one time at the beginning of a row, turn at the end of the previous row and work a slip stitch into each of the stitches to be decreased, then work the appropriate turning chain and continue along the row. To decrease at the end of a row, simply leave the stitches to be decreased unworked, turn, work the appropriate turning chain, and continue along the row.

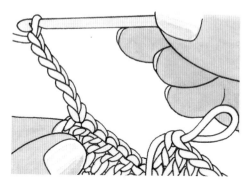

3 To add stitches at the end of a row, leave the last few stitches of the row unworked and remove the hook. Join a length of yarn to the last stitch of the row and work the required number of extra chains, then fasten off the yarn. Insert the hook back into the row and continue, working extra stitches across the chains. Turn and work the next row in the usual way.

EXTERNAL INCREASES AND DECREASES
These have been used to add or subtract groups of stitches at the beginning and end of rows.

INTERNAL INCREASES AND DECREASES
These have been used at the beginning and end of rows to shape the edges. They are commonly used on garments.

CLUSTERS

CLUSTERS ARE GROUPS OF TWO, THREE, OR MORE STITCHES THAT ARE JOINED TOGETHER AT THE TOP BY LEAVING THE LAST LOOP OF EACH STITCH ON THE HOOK, THEN DRAWING THE YARN THROUGH ALL THE LOOPS TO SECURE THE STITCH. THIS TECHNIQUE CAN BE USED AS A WAY OF DECREASING ONE OR MORE STITCHES, BUT CLUSTERS CAN ALSO MAKE ATTRACTIVE STITCH PATTERNS IN THEIR OWN RIGHT.

SEE ALSO

• Shaping, pages 38–39

Tip

Clusters come in different sizes because they can be worked over two, three, or more stitches. Try practicing two-stitch clusters first, then move on to making larger ones.

WORKING A BASIC DOUBLE CROCHET CLUSTER

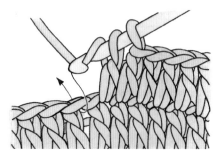

1 To work a two-stitch double crochet cluster, wrap the yarn over the hook and work the first stitch, omitting the last stage to leave two loops on the hook.

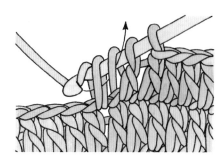

2 Work the last stitch of the cluster in the same way, resulting in three loops on the hook.

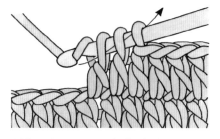

3 Wrap the yarn over the hook, then draw the yarn through all three loops on the hook to complete the cluster and secure the loops.

Stitch collection

Angled clusters

> MULTIPLE OF 5 CHAINS PLUS 4

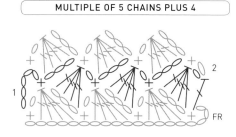

Rows of clusters face in opposite directions, making a beautifully textured crochet fabric. Try working this stitch in two-row stripes of contrasting colors.
NOTE: CL = cluster made from four double crochet stitches worked together (dc4tog).
FOUNDATION ROW: (RS) 1 sc into 4th ch from hook, * ch 3, CL over next 4 chs, ch 1, 1 sc into next ch; rep from * to end, turn.
ROW 1: Ch 5, 1 sc into first CL, * ch 3, CL into next ch 3 sp, ch 1, 1 sc into next CL; rep from * to last ch 3 sp, ch 3, CL into last ch 3 sp, ch 1, 1 dc into last sc, turn.
ROW 2: Ch 1, 1 sc into first CL, * ch 3, CL into next ch 3 sp, ch 1, 1 sc into next CL; rep from * ending last rep with 1 sc into sp made by ch 5, turn.
Rep rows 1 and 2 for length required, ending with a row 2.

Trinity stitch

MULTIPLE OF 2 CHAINS

FR

Trinity stitch is usually worked in one color and the crochet fabric looks the same on both sides, making this stitch ideal for items such as scarves where both sides can be seen.

NOTE: CL = cluster made from three single crochet stitches worked together (sc3tog).

FOUNDATION ROW: 1 sc into 2nd ch from hook, CL inserting hook first into same ch as previous sc, then into each of next 2 chs, * ch 1, CL inserting hook first into same ch as 3rd st of previous CL, then into each of next 2 chs; rep from * to last ch, ch 1, 1 sc into same ch as 3rd st of previous CL, turn.

ROW 1: Ch 1, 1 sc into first sc, ch 1, CL inserting hook first into first ch 1 sp, then into top of next CL, then into next ch 1 sp, * ch 1, CL inserting hook first into same ch 1 sp as 3rd st of previous CL, then into top of next CL, then into next ch 1 sp; rep from * to end working 3rd st of last CL into last sc, 1 sc into same place, turn. Rep row 1 for length required.

Angled clusters

Trinity stitch

SHELL STITCHES

SHELL STITCHES ARE FORMED FROM THREE OR MORE STITCHES THAT SHARE THE SAME CHAIN, STITCH, OR CHAIN SPACE, RESULTING IN A TRIANGULAR GROUP OF STITCHES THAT LOOKS LIKE A CLAM SHELL. USUALLY, CHAINS OR STITCHES AT EITHER SIDE OF A SHELL ARE SKIPPED TO COMPENSATE FOR THE SHELL, AND EACH STITCH MAKING UP A SHELL IS COUNTED AS ONE STITCH. LARGE GROUPS OF STITCHES FORMED INTO SHELLS ARE KNOWN AS FAN STITCHES.

SEE ALSO

• Basic skills and
  stitches, pages 14–21

Tip

When the first row of a stitch pattern requires you to work fairly large shells directly into the foundation chain, it is a good idea to use a size larger hook when making the chain.

WORKING A BASIC DOUBLE CROCHET SHELL

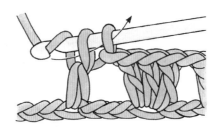

1 Skip the stated number of chains or stitches and work the first double crochet of the shell into the correct chain or stitch.

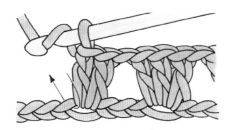

2 Work the second double crochet of the group into the same place as the previous stitch. In the three-stitch shell shown, this stitch forms the center stitch of the shell.

3 Work the remaining stitches of the shell into the same place as the previous stitches.

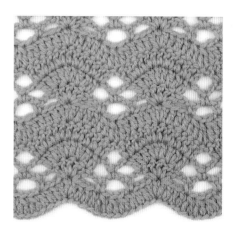

Generous shells

MULTIPLE OF 13 CHAINS PLUS 4

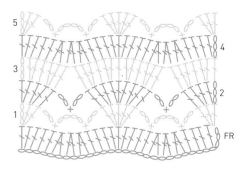

The shell shapes in this large-scale stitch are formed over the course of several rows. Delicate areas of trellis pattern separate each shell to give a lacy touch and lighten the effect.

FOUNDATION ROW: (RS) 1 dc into 4th ch from hook, 1 dc into each of next 3 chs, [dc2tog over next 2 chs] 3 times, 1 dc into each of next 3 chs, * 3 dc into next ch, 1 dc into each of next 3 chs, [dc2tog over next 2 chs] 3 times, 1 dc into each of next 3 chs; rep from * to last ch, 2 dc into last ch, turn.

ROW 1: Ch 3, 2 dc into first dc, ch 2, sk next 3 dc, 1 sc into next dc, ch 4, sk next 3 dc, 1 sc into next dc, ch 2, * sk next 3 dc, 5 dc into next dc, ch 2, sk next 3 dc, 1 sc into next dc, ch 4, sk next 3 dc, 1 sc into next dc, ch 2; rep from * to last 3 dc, sk last 3 dc, 3 dc into beg skipped ch 3, turn.

ROW 2: Ch 3, 1 dc into first dc, 2 dc into next dc, 1 dc into next dc, ch 2, sk next ch 2 sp, 1 sc into next ch 4 sp, ch 2, sk next sc, 1 dc into next dc, 2 dc into next dc, * 3 dc into next dc, 2 dc into next dc, 1 dc into next dc, ch 2, sk next ch 2 sp, 1 sc into next ch 4 sp, ch 2, sk next sc, 1 dc into next dc, 2 dc into next dc; rep from * to turning ch, 2 dc into 3rd of ch 3, turn.

ROW 3: Ch 3, [2 dc into next dc, 1 dc into next dc] twice, sk next sc, 1 dc into next dc, * [2 dc into next dc, 1 dc into next dc] 4 times, sk next sc, 1 dc into next dc; rep from * to last 3 dc, 2 dc into next dc, 1 dc into next dc, 2 dc into last dc, 1 dc into 3rd of ch 3, turn.

ROW 4: Ch 3, 1 dc into each of first 4 dc, [dc2tog over next 2 dc] 3 times, 1 dc into each of next 3 dc, * 3 dc into next dc, 1 dc into each of next 3 dc, [dc2tog over next 2 dc] 3 times, 1 dc into each of next 3 dc; rep from * to turning ch, 2 dc into 3rd of ch 3, turn.

ROW 5: Ch 3, 2 dc into first dc, ch 2, sk next 3 dc, 1 sc into next dc, ch 4, sk next 3 dc, 1 sc into next dc, ch 2, * sk next 3 dc, 5 dc into next dc, ch 2, sk next 3 dc, 1 sc into next dc, ch 4, sk next 3 dc, 1 sc into next dc, ch 2; rep from * to last 3 dc, sk last 3 dc, 3 dc into 3rd of ch 3, turn.
Rep rows 2–5 for length required, ending with a row 4.

Alternate shells

> **MULTIPLE OF 14 CHAINS PLUS 4**

This solidly worked stitch has rows of alternately spaced seven-stitch shells, divided by rows of single crochet. Work this stitch in a solid color or use a hand-painted yarn to get a different look.

FOUNDATION ROW: (RS) 3 dc into 4th ch from hook, * sk next 3 chs, 1 sc into each of next 7 chs, sk next 3 chs, 7 dc into next ch; rep from * ending last rep with 4 dc into last ch, turn.

ROW 1: Ch 1, 1 sc into each st to end working last sc into 3rd of beg skipped ch 3, turn.

ROW 2: Ch 1, 1 sc into each of first 4 sts, sk next 3 sts, 7 dc into next st, sk next 3 sts, 1 sc into each of next 7 sts; rep from * to last 11 sts, sk next 3 sts, 7 dc into next st, sk next 3 sts, 1 sc into each of last 4 sts, sk turning ch 1, turn.

ROW 3: Ch 1, 1 sc into each st to end, sk turning ch 1, turn.

ROW 4: Ch 3, 3 dc into first st, * sk next 3 sts, 1 sc into each of next 7 sts, sk next 3 sts, 7 dc into next st; rep from * ending last rep with 4 dc into last st, sk turning ch 1, turn.

ROW 5: Ch 1, 1 sc into each st to end working last sc into 3rd of ch 3, turn.
Rep rows 2–5 for length required, ending with a row 5.

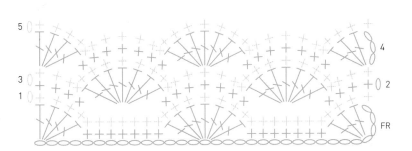

BOBBLES

A BOBBLE IS A GROUP OF STITCHES, USUALLY DOUBLE CROCHET STITCHES, WORKED INTO THE SAME STITCH AT THE BASE AND CLOSED AT THE TOP. WHEN CALCULATING YARN REQUIREMENTS FOR A PROJECT, REMEMBER THAT BOBBLES USE UP MORE YARN THAN MOST OTHER STITCHES.

SEE ALSO

• Basic skills and stitches, pages 14–21

Made from three, four, or five stitches, bobbles are usually worked on wrong side rows and surrounded by flat, solidly worked stitches to throw them into high relief.

WORKING A BASIC FIVE-STITCH BOBBLE

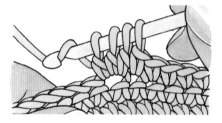

1 On a wrong side row, work to the position of the bobble. Wrap the yarn over the hook and work the first stitch, omitting the last stage to leave two loops on the hook. Work the second and third stitches in the same way. You now have four loops on the hook.

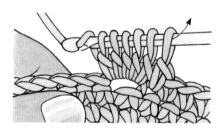

2 Work the remaining two stitches of the bobble in the same way, resulting in six loops on the hook.

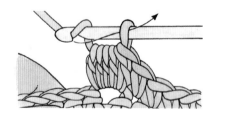

3 Wrap the yarn over the hook and draw it through all six loops to secure them and complete the bobble. As you do so, gently poke the bobble through to the right side with the tip of a finger.

Tip

When working the right side row following a wrong side bobble row, take care to work one stitch into the securing stitch at the top of each bobble.

Stitch collection

All-over bobbles

| MULTIPLE OF 3 CHAINS |

Four-stitch bobbles set against a single crochet background produces a wonderfully textured piece of crochet. This type of stitch is good for making home furnishings such as pillow covers because the fabric is substantial and will keep its shape well.

NOTE: MB = make bobble from four double crochet stitches.

FOUNDATION ROW: (WS) 1 sc into 2nd ch from hook, 1 sc into each ch to end, turn.

ROW 1: Ch 1, 1 sc into each sc to end, turn.

ROW 2: Ch 1, 1 sc into each of first 2 sc, * MB, 1 sc into each of next 2 sc; rep from * to end, turn.

ROW 3: Ch 1, 1 sc into each st to end, turn.

ROW 4: Ch 1, 1 sc into each sc to end, turn. Rep rows 1–4 for length required, ending with a row 4.

Alternate bobbles

MULTIPLE OF 4 CHAINS PLUS 3

All-over bobbles

Make a softer feeling fabric by working a row of double crochet stitches between the bobble rows instead of the more usual single crochet. To make a flatter fabric, simply work three stitches for each bobble instead of four.

NOTE: MB = make bobble from four double crochet stitches.

FOUNDATION ROW: (RS) 1 dc into 4th ch from hook, 1 dc into each ch to end, turn.

ROW 1: Ch 1, 1 sc into each of first 2 dc, * MB, 1 sc into each of next 3 dc; rep from * to last 3 sts, MB, 1 sc into next dc, 1 sc into 3rd of beg skipped ch 3, turn.

ROWS 2 AND 4: Ch 3 (counts as 1 dc), 1 dc into each st to end, turn.

ROW 3: Ch 1, 1 sc into each of first 4 dc, * MB, 1 sc into each of next 3 dc; rep from * ending with 1 sc into 3rd of ch 3, turn.

ROW 5: Ch 1, 1 sc into each of first 2 dc, * MB, 1 sc into each of next 3 dc; rep from * to last 3 sts, MB, 1 sc into next dc, 1 sc into 3rd of ch 3, turn.

Rep rows 2–5 for length required, ending with a row 4.

Alternate bobbles

POPCORNS

A POPCORN IS A CLUSTER OF THREE, FOUR, OR FIVE DOUBLE CROCHET STITCHES THAT IS FOLDED OVER AND CLOSED AT THE TOP WITH A CHAIN. THE POPCORN LOOKS LIKE A TINY FOLDED POCKET THAT STICKS OUT ON THE RIGHT SIDE OF THE CROCHET FABRIC TO GIVE A HIGHLY TEXTURED EFFECT.

SEE ALSO

• Basic skills and stitches, pages 14–21

Tip

If you crochet tightly, you may find it easier to use a size smaller hook to work steps 2 and 3, changing back to the usual size for working each group of double crochet stitches in step 1.

WORKING A BASIC FIVE-STITCH POPCORN

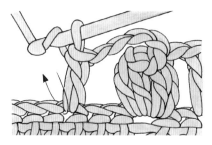

1 Work a group of five double crochet stitches into the same chain or stitch.

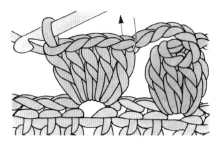

2 Remove the hook from the working loop and insert it under both loops of the first double crochet stitch in the group.

3 To close the popcorn, pick up the working loop with the hook and draw it through to fold the group of stitches and close it at the top. Secure the popcorn by wrapping the yarn over the hook and drawing it through the loop on the hook.

Stitch collection

Lacy popcorns

| MULTIPLE OF 8 CHAINS PLUS 2 |

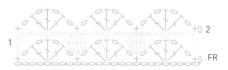

This stitch pattern sets vertical rows of single popcorns against a pretty lacy background, and looks good worked in lighter weights of yarn that will accentuate the delicate structure.

NOTE: PC = popcorn made from five double crochet stitches.

FOUNDATION ROW: (RS) 1 sc into 2nd ch from hook, * ch 1, sk next 3 chs, [1 dc, ch 1, 1 dc, ch 1, 1 dc, ch 1] into next ch, sk next 3 chs, 1 sc into next ch; rep from * to end, turn.

ROW 1: Ch 6 (counts as 1 dc, ch 3), sk first dc, 1 sc into next dc, * ch 3, PC into next sc, ch 3, sk next dc, 1 sc into next dc; rep from * to last sc, ch 3, 1 dc into last sc, turn.

ROW 2: Ch 1, 1 sc into first dc, * ch 1, [1 dc, ch 1, 1 dc, ch 1, 1 dc] into next sc, ch 1, 1 sc into top of next PC; rep from * to end working last sc into 3rd of ch 6, turn. Rep rows 1 and 2 for length required, ending with a row 2.

Popcorn columns

MULTIPLE OF 11 CHAINS PLUS 5

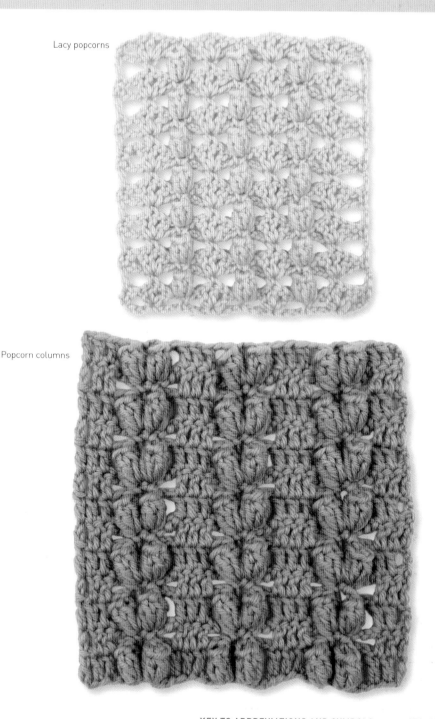

This is a much heavier stitch than the lacy popcorns, but still makes a crochet fabric with good drape. Use this stitch for making throws and afghans where you need a textured surface.

NOTE: PC = popcorn made from five double crochet stitches.

FOUNDATION ROW: (RS) 1 dc into 4th ch from hook, 1 dc into next ch, * ch 2, sk next 3 chs, PC into next ch, ch 1, PC into next ch, ch 1, sk next 3 chs, 1 dc into each of next 3 chs; rep from * to end, turn.

ROW 1: Ch 3, sk first dc, 1 dc into each of next 2 dc, * ch 3, sk next ch and PC, 2 sc into ch 1 sp between PCs, ch 3, sk next PC and 2 chs, 1 dc into each of next 3 dc; rep from * to end working last dc into 3rd of beg skipped ch 3, turn.

ROW 2: Ch 3, sk first dc, 1 dc into each of next 2 dc, * ch 2, sk next 3 chs, PC into next sc, ch 1, PC into next sc, ch 1, sk next 3 chs, 1 dc into each of next 3 dc; rep from * to end working last dc into 3rd of ch 3, turn.

ROW 3: Ch 3, sk first dc, 1 dc into each of next 2 dc, * ch 3, sk next ch and PC, 2 sc into ch 1 sp between PCs, ch 3, sk next PC and 2 chs, 1 dc into each of next 3 dc; rep from * to end working last dc into 3rd of ch 3, turn.

Rep rows 2 and 3 for length required, ending with a row 2.

Lacy popcorns

Popcorn columns

PUFF STITCHES

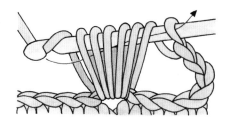

PUFF STITCHES ARE SOFT, FLUFFY GROUPS OF STITCHES THAT ARE LESS TEXTURED THAN EITHER BOBBLES OR POPCORNS. A PUFF STITCH IS MADE FROM THREE OR MORE HALF DOUBLE CROCHET STITCHES THAT ARE WORKED INTO THE SAME CHAIN OR STITCH. PUFF STITCHES NEED A LITTLE PRACTICE TO WORK SUCCESSFULLY.

SEE ALSO
- Bobbles, pages 44–45
- Popcorns, pages 46–47

WORKING A BASIC PUFF STITCH

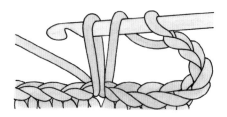

1 Wrap the yarn over the hook, insert the hook into the specified chain or stitch, wrap the yarn over the hook again, and draw a loop through so that there are three loops on the hook.

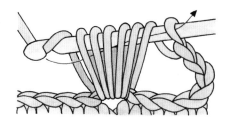

2 Repeat step 1 twice more, each time inserting the hook into the same place, so that there are seven loops on the hook. Wrap the yarn over the hook again and draw it through all the loops on the hook.

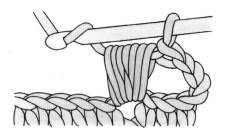

3 A chain stitch is often worked to close the puff stitch and secure the loops. Wrap the yarn over the hook and draw it through the loop on the hook to complete the securing chain stitch.

Tip

Puff stitches can be a little tricky to work, especially for a beginner. It is a good idea to practice them using a smooth, bulky yarn and large hook until you understand the stitch construction.

Stitch collection

Puff stitch stripes

MULTIPLE OF 2 CHAINS PLUS 2

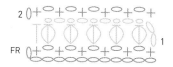

This stitch makes a softly textured crochet fabric that is perfect for making baby blankets and small afghans when worked in baby yarn. You can use either side of the work as the right side.

NOTE: PS = puff stitch made from three half double crochet stitches closed with one chain stitch.

FOUNDATION ROW: 1 sc into 2nd ch from hook, * ch 1, sk next ch, 1 sc into next ch; rep from * to end, turn.

ROW 1: Ch 2 (counts as 1 hdc), * PS into next ch 1 sp, ch 1, sk next sc; rep from * to last ch 1 sp, PS into last ch 1 sp, 1 hdc into last sc, turn.

ROW 2: Ch 1, 1 sc into first hdc, * ch 1, sk next st, 1 sc into next ch 1 sp; rep from * to end working last sc into 2nd of ch 2, turn.

Rep rows 1 and 2 for length required, ending with a row 2.

Puff stitch waves

MULTIPLE OF 17 CHAINS PLUS 2

Puff stitches combined with groups of decreases make this pretty ripple pattern. It looks attractive worked in a solid color or in two-row stripes of closely toning colors.

NOTE: PS = puff stitch made from three half double crochet stitches closed with one chain stitch.

dc2tog = work two double crochet stitches together.

FOUNDATION ROW: (RS) 1 dc into 4th ch from hook, [dc2tog over next 2 chs] twice, * [ch 1, PS into next ch] 5 times, ch 1, ** [dc2tog over next 2 chs] 6 times; rep from * ending last rep at ** when 6 chs rem, [dc2tog over next 2 chs] 3 times, turn.

ROW 1: Ch 1, 1 sc into each st and ch 1 sp to end excluding beg skipped ch 3, turn.

ROW 2: Ch 3, sk first sc, 1 dc into next sc, [dc2tog over next 2 sc] twice, * [ch 1, PS into next sc] 5 times, ch 1, ** [dc2tog over next 2 sc] 6 times; rep from * ending last rep at ** when 6 sc rem, [dc2tog over next 2 sc] 3 times, sk turning ch 1, turn.

Rep rows 2 and 3 for length required, ending with a row 2.

Puff stitch stripes

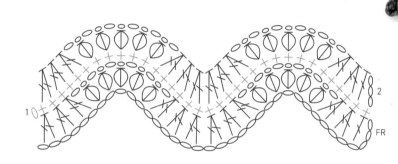

Puff stitch waves

LOOP STITCHES

LOOP STITCHES FALL INTO TWO CATEGORIES. THE FIRST IS WHERE EXTENDED LOOPS ARE MADE FROM THE WORKING YARN (LOOP STITCH). THE SECOND IS WHERE SHORT LENGTHS OF CROCHET CHAIN ARE FORMED INTO LOOPS (ASTRAKHAN STITCH). BOTH TYPES OF STITCH MAKE A DELIGHTFUL TEXTURE AND ARE GOOD FOR MAKING ACCESSORIES SUCH AS SCARVES AND HATS, OR FOR WORKING COLLARS AND CUFFS TO TRIM A PLAIN GARMENT.

SEE ALSO
• Basic skills and stitches, pages 14–21

WORKING A LOOP STITCH

Loop stitches are often worked on wrong side rows of single crochet by extending a loop of yarn with your finger. You may need some practice before you are able to make all the loops the same size. Loop stitches can be worked into every stitch along the row.

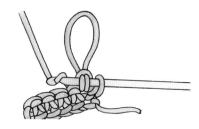

1 With the wrong side of the work facing you, insert the hook into the next stitch as usual. Using one finger, pull up the working yarn to make a loop of the desired size, pick up both strands of the loop with the hook, and draw them through the crochet fabric.

2 Take your finger out of the yarn loop and wrap the working yarn over the hook.

3 Carefully draw the yarn through all three loops on the hook.

WORKING ASTRAKHAN STITCH

Astrakhan stitch is worked back and forth without turning the work. Loops of crochet chain are made on right side rows by working into the front loops of the previous plain row. Each following plain row is worked into the back loops of the previous plain row.

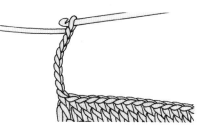

1 **PLAIN ROW:** Work a row of double crochet stitches. At the end of the row, work the number of chains specified in the pattern. Do not turn.

2 **LOOP ROW:** Working from left to right, and keeping the crochet chain behind the hook, work a slip stitch into the front loop of the next double crochet made on the previous row. Repeat along the row and do not turn at the end of the row.

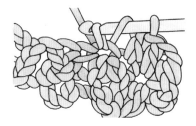

3 **PLAIN ROW:** Working from right to left behind the chain loops made on the previous row, work a double crochet stitch into the back loop of each stitch made on the first plain row.

Stitch collection

Banded loop stitch

MULTIPLE OF 8 CHAINS PLUS 2

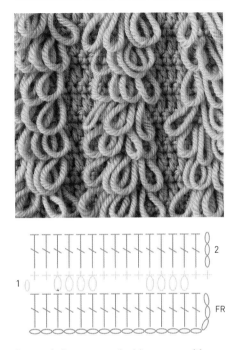

Loop stitches are worked in groups of four to make vertical bands of texture that contrast well with the plain background.

FOUNDATION ROW: (RS) 1 dc into 4th ch from hook, 1 dc into each ch to end, turn.

ROW 1: Ch 1, 1 sc into each of first 2 dc, * loop stitch into each of next 4 dc, 1 sc into each of next 4 dc; rep from * to last 6 sts, loop stitch into each of next 4 dc, 1 sc into next dc, 1 sc into 3rd of beg skipped ch 3, turn.

ROW 2: Ch 3 (counts as 1 dc), 1 dc into each st to end, sk turning ch 1, turn.

Rep rows 1 and 2 for length required, ending with a row 1.

Astrakhan stitch

ANY NUMBER OF CHAINS PLUS 2

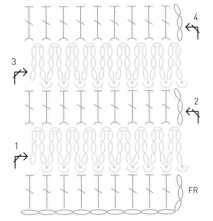

Loops of crochet chains are worked on alternate rows to create this highly textured stitch. It is worked without turning at the end of the rows.

FOUNDATION ROW: (RS) 1 dc into 4th ch from hook, 1 dc into each ch to end. Do not turn.

ROW 1: (LOOP ROW) Working from left to right, sk first dc, * ch 7, sl st into front loop of next dc to right; rep from * to end working last sl st into both loops of 3rd of beg skipped ch 3. Do not turn.

ROW 2: (PLAIN ROW) Working from right to left behind loops made on previous row, ch 3, sk first st, * 1 dc into back loop of next dc worked on foundation row; rep from * to end. Do not turn.

ROW 3: (LOOP ROW) Working from left to right, * ch 7, sk first dc, sl st into front loop of next dc to right; rep from * to end working last sl st into both loops of 3rd of ch 3. Do not turn.

ROW 4: (PLAIN ROW) Working from right to left behind loops made on previous row, ch 3, sk first st, * 1 dc into back loop of next dc worked on last but one row; rep from * to end. Do not turn.

Rep rows 3 and 4 for length required, ending with a row 4.

OPENWORK AND LACE STITCHES

THESE VERSATILE STITCHES CAN BE USED TO MAKE ACCESSORIES SUCH AS SHAWLS AND WRAPS, AS WELL AS LIGHTWEIGHT, SIMPLY SHAPED SUMMER GARMENTS. THEY ARE STRAIGHTFORWARD TO WORK, BUT IT IS ESSENTIAL TO MAKE THE CORRECT NUMBER OF CHAINS IN THE FOUNDATION CHAIN.

SEE ALSO

- Basic skills and stitches, pages 14–21
- Surface crochet, pages 112–113

WORKING A TRELLIS PATTERN

Although similar in construction, trellis patterns have longer chain spaces than mesh patterns, with the chain spaces curving upward to create delicate arches. The chain spaces are usually anchored by single crochet stitches worked into the space below each arch.

PLAIN TRELLIS WORKED IN THE ROUND

The number of chain stitches in each loop increases by one chain stitch for each new round.

WORKING A MESH PATTERN

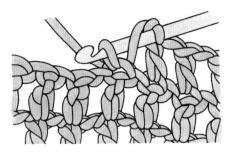

1 When working a mesh pattern, take care to insert the hook into the correct place. In this example, the hook is inserted into the top of each stitch made on the previous row.

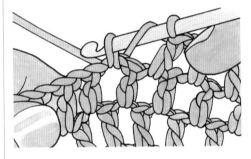

2 Some mesh patterns are made by inserting the hook into the chain spaces between stitches worked on the previous row. Do not insert the hook directly into the chain, but into the space below it.

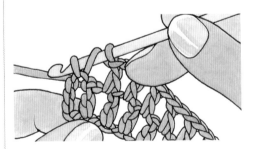

3 When working the last stitch of the row, work it into the third stitch of the turning chain rather than into the chain space. This makes a neater, more stable edge.

Stitch collection

Plain trellis

MULTIPLE OF 4 CHAINS PLUS 2

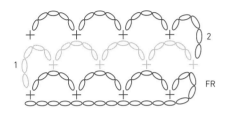

This easy-to-work stitch is lovely when used to make a lightweight wrap, scarf, or stole. It is reversible, so you can choose which side you prefer as the right side.

FOUNDATION ROW: 1 sc into 6th ch from hook, * ch 5, sk next 3 chs, 1 sc into next ch; rep from * to end, turn.

ROW 1: * Ch 5, 1 sc into next ch 5 sp; rep from * to end, turn.

Rep row 1 for length required.

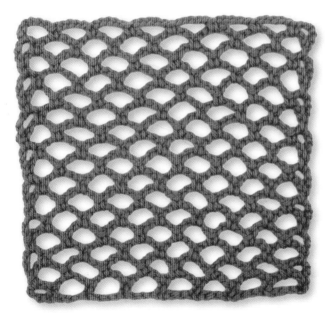

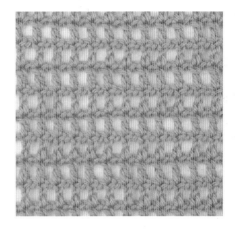

Openwork mesh

MULTIPLE OF 2 CHAINS PLUS 4

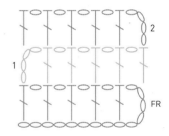

This stitch is very easy to work and is a good introduction to openwork stitch patterns for the beginner. It also makes a good background stitch for surface crochet.

FOUNDATION ROW: (RS) 1 dc into 6th ch from hook, * ch 1, sk next ch, 1 dc into next ch; rep from * to end, turn.

ROW 1: Ch 4 (counts as 1 dc, ch 1), * 1 dc into next dc, ch 1; rep from * to end working last dc into 2nd of beg skipped ch 5, turn.

ROW 2: Ch 4 (counts as 1 dc, ch 1), * 1 dc into next dc, ch 1; rep from * to end working last dc into 3rd of ch 3, turn.

Rep row 2 for length required.

Stitch collection

Fancy openwork

MULTIPLE OF 18 CHAINS PLUS 8

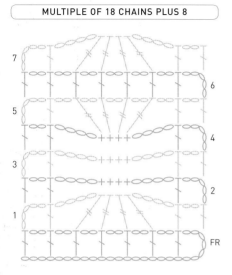

A more challenging stitch to work than either of the previous ones, the resulting crochet fabric is soft and delicate with good drape. Choose which side you prefer as the right side.

FOUNDATION ROW: 1 dc into 8th ch from hook, * ch 2, sk next 2 chs, 1 dc into next ch; rep from * to end, turn.

ROW 1: Ch 5 (counts as 1 dc, ch 2), sk first dc, 1 dc into next dc, * ch 4, 1 tr into each of next 4 dc, ch 4, 1 dc into next dc, ch 2, 1 dc into next dc; rep from * to end working last dc into 3rd of beg skipped ch 7, turn.

ROW 2: Ch 5, sk first dc, 1 dc into next dc, * ch 4, 1 sc into each of next 4 tr, ch 4, 1 dc into next dc, ch 2, 1 dc into next dc; rep from * to end working last dc into 3rd of ch 5, turn.

ROWS 3 AND 4: Ch 5, sk first dc, 1 dc into next dc, * ch 4, 1 sc into each of next 4 sc, ch 4, 1 dc into next dc, ch 2, 1 dc into next dc; rep from * to end working last dc into 3rd of ch 5, turn.

ROW 5: Ch 5, sk first dc, 1 dc into next dc, * ch 2, [1 tr into next sc, ch 2] 4 times, 1 dc into next dc, ch 2, 1 dc into next dc; rep from * to end working last dc into 3rd of ch 5, turn.

ROW 6: Ch 5, sk first dc, 1 dc into next dc, * ch 2, [1 dc into next tr, ch 2] 4 times, 1 dc into next dc, ch 2, 1 dc into next dc; rep from * to end working last dc into 3rd of ch 5, turn.

ROW 7: Ch 5, sk first dc, 1 dc into next dc, * ch 4, 1 tr into each of next 4 dc, ch 4, 1 dc into next dc, ch 2, 1 dc into next dc; rep from * to end working last dc into 3rd of ch 5, turn.

Rep rows 2–7 for length required, ending with a row 6.

Fancy openwork

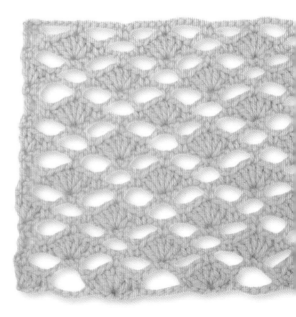

Seashore trellis

Seashore trellis

> MULTIPLE OF 12 CHAINS PLUS 4

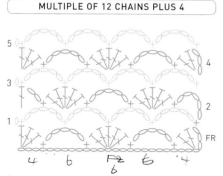

A combination of a trellis pattern and shell stitches, this stitch works well for a scarf or baby shawl. Choose a lightweight yarn to enhance the beauty of the stitch pattern.

FOUNDATION ROW: (RS) 2 dc into 4th ch from hook, * sk next 2 chs, 1 sc into next ch, ch 5, sk next 5 chs, 1 sc into next ch, sk next 2 chs, 5 dc into next ch; rep from * to end working only 3 dc into last ch, turn.

ROW 1: Ch 1, 1 sc into first dc, * ch 5, 1 sc into next ch 5 sp, ch 5, 1 sc into 3rd dc of next 5 dc group; rep from * to end working last sc into 3rd of beg skipped ch 3, turn.

ROW 2: * Ch 5, 1 sc into next ch 5 sp, 5 dc into next sc, 1 sc into next ch 5 sp; rep from * ending with ch 2, 1 dc into last sc, turn.

ROW 3: Ch 1, 1 sc into first dc, * ch 5, 1 sc into 3rd dc of next 5 dc group, ch 5, 1 sc into next ch 5 sp; rep from * to end, turn.

ROW 4: Ch 3, 2 dc into first sc, * 1 sc into next ch 5 sp, ch 5, 1 sc into next ch 5 sp, 5 dc into next sc; rep from * to end working only 3 dc into last sc, turn.

ROW 5: Ch 1, 1 sc into first dc, * ch 5, 1 sc into next ch 5 sp, ch 5, 1 sc into 3rd dc of next 5 dc group; rep from * to end working last sc into 3rd of ch 3, turn.

Rep rows 2–5 for length required, ending with a row 4.

Fan lace

> MULTIPLE OF 12 CHAINS PLUS 3

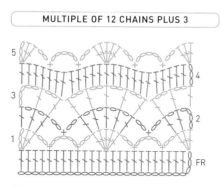

This attractive, large-scale lace pattern is deceptively easy to work in single and double crochet stitches. Work it in a soft cotton or cotton blend yarn to make a pretty wrap to wear on summer evenings.

FOUNDATION ROW: (RS) 1 dc into 4th ch from hook, 1 dc into each ch to end, turn.

ROW 1: Ch 3, 2 dc into first dc, ch 2, sk next 3 dc, 1 sc into next dc, ch 5, sk next 3 dc, 1 sc into next dc, ch 2, sk next 3 dc, * 5 dc into next dc, ch 2, sk next 3 dc, 1 sc into next dc, ch 5, sk next 3 dc, 1 sc into next dc, ch 2, sk next 3 dc; rep from * ending with 3 dc into 3rd of beg skipped ch 3, turn.

ROW 2: Ch 4, sk first dc, 1 dc into next dc, ch 1, 1 dc into next dc, ch 2, sk next ch 2 sp, 1 sc into next ch 5 sp, ch 2, * [1 dc into next dc, ch 1] 4 times, 1 dc into next dc, ch 2, sk next ch 2 sp, 1 sc into next ch 5 sp, ch 2; rep from * to last 2 dc, [1 dc into next dc, ch 1] twice, 1 dc into 3rd of ch 3, turn.

ROW 3: Ch 5, sk first dc, 1 dc into next dc, ch 2, 1 dc into next dc, * sk next sc, [1 dc into next dc, ch 2] 4 times, 1 dc into next dc; rep from * to last sc, sk last sc, [1 dc into next dc, ch 2] twice, 1 dc into 3rd of ch 4, turn.

ROW 4: Ch 3, 2 dc into next ch 2 sp, 1 dc into next dc, 2 dc into next ch 2 sp, sk next dc, 1 dc into next dc, * [2 dc into next ch 2 sp, 1 dc into next dc] 3 times, 2 dc into next

ch 2 sp, sk next dc, 1 dc into next dc; rep from * to last ch 2 sp, 2 dc into last ch 2 sp, 1 dc into next dc, 2 dc into sp formed by ch 5, sk first 2 chs of ch 5, 1 dc into 3rd of ch 5, turn.

ROW 5: Ch 3, 2 dc into first dc, ch 2, sk next 3 dc, 1 sc into next dc, ch 5, sk next 3 dc, 1 sc into next dc, ch 2, sk next 3 dc, * 5 dc into next dc, ch 2, sk next 3 dc, 1 sc into next dc, ch 5, sk next 3 dc, 1 sc into next dc, ch 2, sk next 3 dc; rep from * ending with 3 dc into 3rd of ch 3, turn.

Rep rows 2–5 for length required, ending with a row 4.

KEY TO ABBREVIATIONS AND SYMBOLS **pages 150–151**

FILET CROCHET

FILET CROCHET IS AN OPENWORK TYPE OF CROCHET CHARACTERIZED BY A MESH BACKGROUND ON WHICH THE PATTERN IS PICKED OUT IN SOLID BLOCKS OF STITCHES. IT IS TRADITIONALLY WORKED IN FINE COTTON THREAD, BUT ALSO LOOKS EFFECTIVE WORKED IN YARN.

SEE ALSO
• Openwork and lace stitches, pages 52–55

FILET CROCHET PATTERNS

Filet crochet patterns are always worked from a chart that shows the pattern as it will appear on the right side of the work. The chart rows are numbered at the sides, and you follow the numbered sequence, working upward from the bottom of the chart (row 1) and from side to side (see diagram below).

A filet crochet "unit" comprises a beginning double crochet, either two chains for a space or two double crochet stitches for a block, and an ending double crochet. The ending double crochet stitch is also the beginning double crochet of the next unit.

HEART MOTIF
Filet crochet lends itself to working simplified motifs such as this heart, which can be worked as a single motif or turned on its side and repeated to make a lovely border.

WORKING THE FIRST ROW

Filet crochet charts begin with the first row, so the foundation chain is not shown. To calculate the number of chains to make, you will need to multiply the number of squares across the chart by three and add one. For example, for a chart that is 20 squares across, make a foundation chain 61 chains long (20 x 3 + 1). You also need to add the correct number of turning chains, depending on whether the first chart row begins with a space or a block. After making the foundation chain, start to follow the chart from the bottom right-hand corner, working along the row of squares marked 1. Follow the directions for the first square, depending on whether the first square is a space or a block.

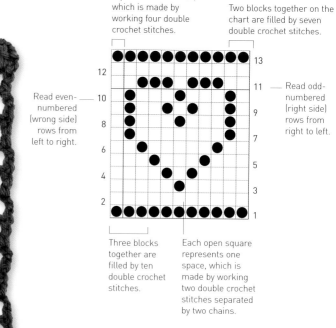

Each filled square represents one block, which is made by working four double crochet stitches.

Two blocks together on the chart are filled by seven double crochet stitches.

Read even-numbered (wrong side) rows from left to right.

Read odd-numbered (right side) rows from right to left.

Three blocks together are filled by ten double crochet stitches.

Each open square represents one space, which is made by working two double crochet stitches separated by two chains.

STARTING THE FIRST ROW WITH A SPACE

When the first square is a space, add four turning chains and work the first double crochet stitch into the eighth chain from the hook. Continue working spaces and blocks along the row, reading the chart from right to left.

STARTING THE FIRST ROW WITH A BLOCK

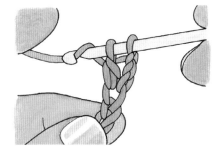

1 When the first square on the chart is a block, add two turning chains and work the first double crochet stitch into the fourth chain from the hook.

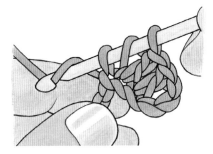

2 Work one double crochet stitch into each of the next two chains to complete the first block. Continue along the row, reading the chart from right to left.

WORKING THE REST OF THE CHART ROWS

At the end of the first row, turn the work and follow the second row of the chart, reading from left to right. Work spaces and blocks at the beginning and end of the second and subsequent rows as follows.

WORKING A SPACE OVER A SPACE ON THE PREVIOUS ROW

1 At the beginning of a row, work five turning chains (these count as one double crochet stitch and two chains), skip the first stitch and the next two chains, then work one double crochet stitch into the next double crochet stitch. Continue across the row, working the spaces and blocks from the chart.

2 At the end of a row, finish by working one double crochet stitch into the last double crochet stitch, then work two chains, skip two chains, and work one double crochet stitch into the third of the five turning chains, then turn.

WORKING A SPACE OVER A BLOCK ON THE PREVIOUS ROW

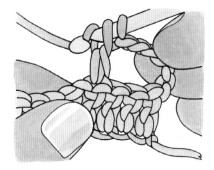

1 At the beginning of a row, work five turning chains (these count as one double crochet stitch and two chains), skip the first three stitches, then work one double crochet stitch into the next double crochet stitch. Continue across the row, working spaces and blocks from the chart.

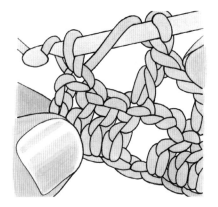

2 At the end of a row, work to the last four stitches. Work one double crochet stitch into the next stitch, work two chains, skip two stitches, and work one double crochet stitch into the top of the three turning chains to complete the block, then turn.

Stitch collection

WORKING A BLOCK OVER A SPACE ON THE PREVIOUS ROW

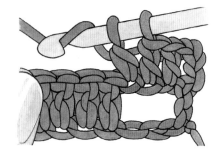

1 At the beginning of a row, work three turning chains (these count as one double crochet stitch), then skip one stitch, work one double crochet stitch into each of the next two chains, and one double crochet stitch into the next stitch to complete the block. Continue across the row working spaces and blocks from the chart.

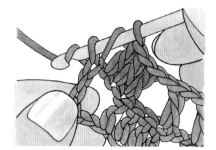

2 At the end of a row, finish by working one double crochet stitch into the last double crochet stitch and one double crochet stitch into each of the next three chains of the turning chain, then turn.

WORKING A BLOCK OVER A BLOCK ON THE PREVIOUS ROW

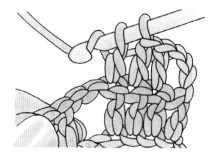

1 At the beginning of a row, work three turning chains (these count as one double crochet stitch), then skip one stitch and work one double crochet stitch into each of the next three double crochet stitches to complete the block. Continue across the row working spaces and blocks from the chart.

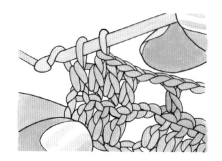

2 At the end of a row, finish by working one double crochet stitch into each of the last three double crochet stitches and one double crochet stitch into the top of the three turning chains, then turn.

Checkerboard

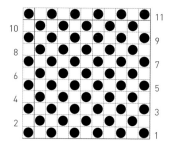

This pattern is one of the simplest designs for filet crochet, consisting of alternating blocks and spaces. It is a great, easy-to-work stitch for making lightweight blankets and throws.

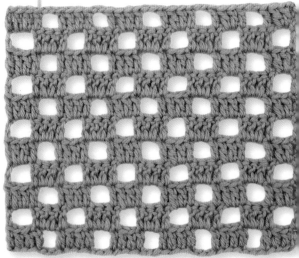

Tiny flowers

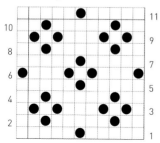

This design has a lighter feel than the checkerboard pattern. Groups of four blocks are arranged to make stylized flowers at regular intervals across the plain mesh background.

Sitting cat

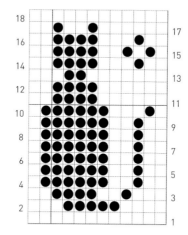

This cat motif would look pretty repeated several times across the border of a baby shawl or snuggle blanket. Use a lightweight baby yarn and a fairly small hook to make the most of the design.

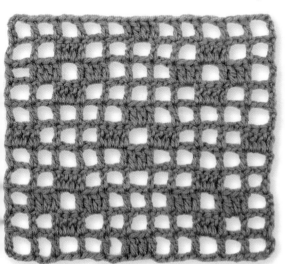

CHEVRON PATTERNS

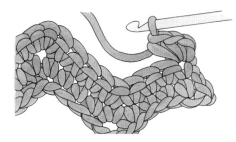

CHEVRON PATTERNS ARE WORKED IN A SIMILAR WAY TO PLAIN HORIZONTAL STRIPES, BUT IN THIS TYPE OF STRIPE PATTERN EXTRA STITCHES ARE ADDED AND SUBTRACTED AT REGULAR INTERVALS ALONG EACH ROW.

SEE ALSO
- Basic skills and stitches, pages 14–21
- Stripe patterns, pages 34–35

The adding and subtracting of stitches forms a pattern of regular peaks and troughs, separated by blocks of stitches, and creates attractive patterns often known as ripple patterns. The peaks and troughs can form sharp points or gentle waves, depending on the pattern, and the effect can vary when the number of stitches in the blocks between the peaks and troughs is changed.

With basic chevron patterns, the pattern repeat is usually set on the first row after you have worked the foundation row of stitches into the foundation chain. This row is then repeated until the work is the required length. More complex chevron patterns, combining smooth, textured, and lace stitches, are made up of peaks and troughs in a similar way, but each pattern repeat may take several rows to complete. Join new colors at the end of rows in the same way as when working simple stripe patterns.

CHEVRON EDGING

Working one or two rows of a chevron pattern creates a useful edging, such as this two-row single crochet chevron pattern (see step-by-step sequence, right).

RIC RAC EDGING

To create this ric rac pattern, work three single crochet stitches into one chain, one single crochet into the next chain, then skip the following chain and work one single crochet stitch into the chain after that. Repeat this sequence to the end of the chain. This edging, worked in fine cotton, is ideal for trimming fabric projects.

WORKING A CHEVRON PATTERN IN SINGLE CROCHET

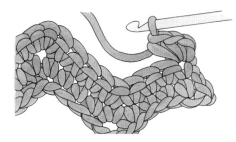

1 To keep the peaks and troughs of chevron stripe patterns correctly spaced, you may need to work one or more extra stitches at the beginning or end (or both) of every row. In this easy pattern, two single crochet stitches are worked into the first stitch of every row.

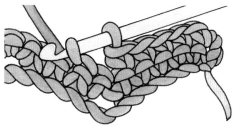

2 To make the bottom V-shapes of the chevron pattern (the troughs), skip two single crochet stitches (sk next 2 sc) at the bottom of the troughs, then continue working the next block of stitches.

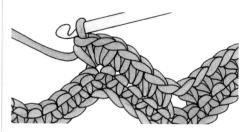

3 To make the top V-shapes of the chevrons (the peaks), work three single crochet stitches into the same stitch (3 sc into next sc) at the top of the peaks.

Stitch collection

Single crochet chevrons

MULTIPLE OF 11 CHAINS PLUS 2

YARN: Worked in three colors, A, B, and C. Using yarn A, make the required length of foundation chain.

FOUNDATION ROW: (RS) 2 sc into 2nd ch from hook, * 1 sc into each of next 4 chs, sk next 2 chs, 1 sc into each of next 4 chs, 3 sc into next ch; rep from * ending last rep with 2 sc into last ch, turn.

ROW 1: Ch 1, 2 sc into first sc, * 1 sc into each of next 4 sc, sk next 2 sc, 1 sc into each of next 4 sc, 3 sc into next sc; rep from * ending last rep with 2 sc into last sc, turn.

Rep row 1, changing yarns in the following color sequence:

        4 rows in yarn A
        4 rows in yarn B
        4 rows in yarn C

Repeat for length required.

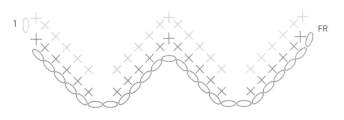

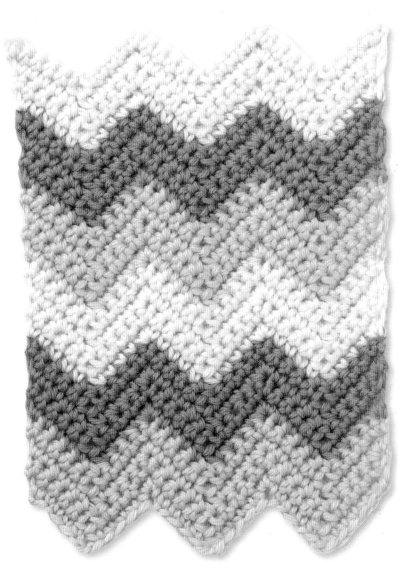

WORKING A CHEVRON PATTERN IN DOUBLE CROCHET

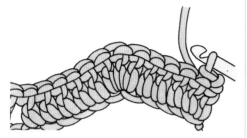

1 Instead of working extra stitches at the beginning of a row, you may be instructed to work one or more slip stitches in order to move the yarn and hook to the correct place for working the row. In this pattern, turn and work a slip stitch into the second double crochet stitch of the row (sl st into 2nd dc) before working the turning chain.

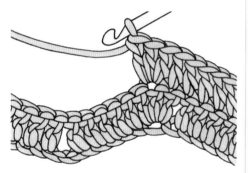

2 Three stitches are worked into the same stitch on the previous row to form the peaks. Work the block of stitches before the peak, then work three double crochet stitches into the next double crochet stitch (3 dc into next dc). The troughs are made in the same way as the single crochet pattern (see page 60), by simply skipping two stitches at the bottom of the troughs.

WORKING A WAVE PATTERN IN DOUBLE CROCHET

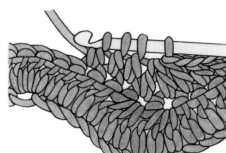

1 Soft waves are made by working two sets of increases and decreases into the peaks and troughs instead of one. To make the troughs, work three double crochet stitches together over the six stitches (dc3tog over next 6 sts) at the bottom of each trough.

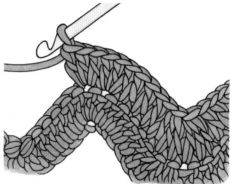

2 To make the peaks, work three double crochet stitches into each of the central two stitches (3 dc into each of next 2 dc) at the top of the peaks.

Double crochet chevrons

MULTIPLE OF 13 CHAINS

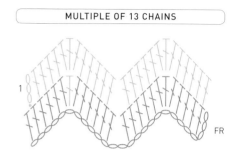

1

FR

YARN: Worked in two colors, A and B. Using yarn A, make the required length of foundation chain.

FOUNDATION ROW: (RS) 1 dc into 4th ch from hook, 1 dc into each of next 3 chs, * 3 dc into next ch, 1 dc into each of next 5 chs, sk next 2 chs, 1 dc into each of next 5 chs; rep from * to last 6 chs, 3 dc into next ch, 1 dc into each of next 5 chs, turn.

ROW 1: Sl st into 2nd dc, ch 3, 1 dc into each of next 4 dc, * 3 dc into next dc, 1 dc into each of next 5 dc, sk next 2 dc, 1 dc into each of next 5 dc; rep from * to last 6 sts, 3 dc into next dc, 1 dc into each of next 5 dc, turn.

Rep row 1, changing yarns in the following color sequence:

2 rows in yarn A
2 rows in yarn B

Repeat for length required.

Wavy chevrons

> ## MULTIPLE OF 14 CHAINS PLUS 3

YARN: Worked in three colors, A, B, and C. Using yarn A, make the required length of foundation chain.

FOUNDATION ROW: (RS) 2 dc into 4th ch from hook, 1 dc into each of next 3 chs, [dc3tog over next 3 chs] twice, 1 dc into each of next 3 chs, * 3 dc into each of next 2 chs, 1 dc into each of next 3 chs, [dc3tog over next 3 chs] twice, 1 dc into each of next 3 chs; rep from * to last ch, 3 dc into last ch, turn.

ROW 1: Ch 3, 2 dc into first dc, 1 dc into each of next 3 dc, dc3tog twice, 1 dc into each of next 3 dc, * 3 dc into each of next 2 dc, 1 dc into each of next 3 dc, dc3tog twice, 1 dc into each of next 3 dc; rep from * to beg skipped chs, 3 dc into 3rd of beg skipped ch 3, turn.

Join yarn B but do not break off yarn A.

ROW 2: Ch 3, 2 dc into first dc, 1 dc into each of next 3 dc, dc3tog twice, 1 dc into each of next 3 dc, * 3 dc into each of next 2 dc, 1 dc into each of next 3 dc, dc3tog twice, 1 dc into each of next 3 dc; rep from * to turning ch, 3 dc into 3rd of ch 3, turn.

Rep row 2, changing yarns in the following color sequence:

1 row (foundation row) in yarn A
[1A, 1B, 1A, 1C, 2A] rep to end
Repeat for length required.

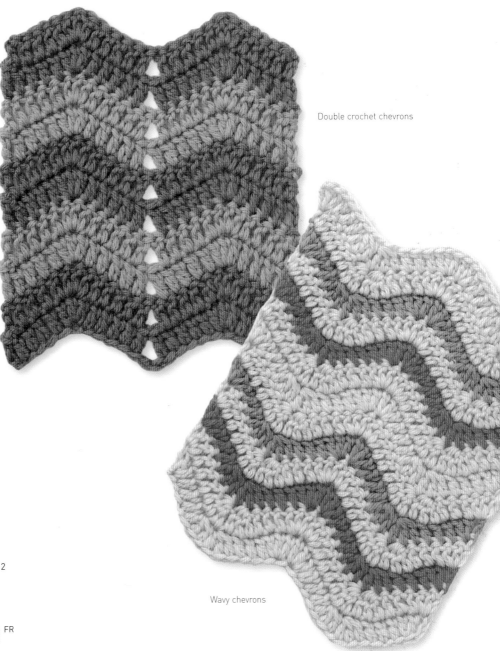

Double crochet chevrons

Wavy chevrons

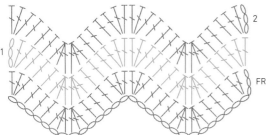

KEY TO ABBREVIATIONS AND SYMBOLS pages 150–151

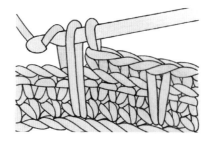

SPIKE STITCHES

SPIKE STITCHES (ALSO CALLED DROPPED STITCHES) ARE WORKED OVER THE TOP OF OTHER STITCHES TO ADD COLOR OR TEXTURE TO CROCHET. THE STITCHES ARE WORKED SINGLY OR IN GROUPS OVER ONE OR MORE ROWS, AND ARE USUALLY WORKED IN SINGLE CROCHET.

SEE ALSO

• Stripe patterns, pages 34–35

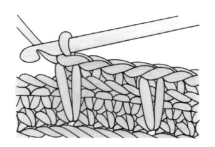

FABRIC WEIGHT
Spike stitches create a thick fabric.

As well as making interesting color patterns when worked in two or more contrasting colors, spike stitches also create a thick, densely worked fabric, without very much drape, which is good for making adult outerwear and accessories such as hats, purses, and bags.

WORKING A BASIC SINGLE CROCHET SPIKE STITCH

1 Insert the hook into the work the specified number of rows below the next stitch as directed in the pattern instructions, taking the point right through the fabric to the wrong side. Wrap the yarn over the hook and draw through, lengthening the loop to the height of the working row.

2 To finish the spike, complete the stitch in the usual way. When working spike stitches, take care not to pull the loop too tight because this will distort the fabric.

Stitch collection

Spiked stripes

MULTIPLE OF 8 CHAINS PLUS 1

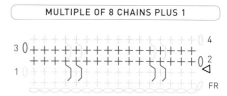

Stripes of contrasting colors show off spike stitches to perfection. In this stitch, the color changes after every two rows, with the color not in use being carried loosely up the side to avoid lots of yarn ends.

YARN: Worked in two colors, A and B.

NOTE: SP = spike stitch made by inserting hook into work two rows below next stitch and working a single crochet stitch.

Using yarn A, make the required length of foundation chain.

FOUNDATION ROW: (RS) 1 sc into 2nd ch from hook, 1 sc into each ch to end, turn.

ROW 1: Ch 1, 1 sc into each sc to end, turn. Join yarn B but do not break off yarn A.

ROW 2: Using yarn B, ch 1, * 1 sc into each of next 3 sc, SP twice, 1 sc into each of next 3 sc; rep from * to end, turn.

ROW 3: Using yarn B, ch 1, 1 sc into each sc to end, turn.

ROW 4: Using yarn A, ch 1, * 1 sc into each of next 3 sc, SP twice, 1 sc into each of next 3 sc; rep from * to end, turn.

Rep rows 1–4 for length required, ending with a row 1.

Tip

When first trying out spike stitches, it is easier to see exactly what is happening if you work each row using a contrasting color of yarn.

Alternate spikes

MULTIPLE OF 2 CHAINS

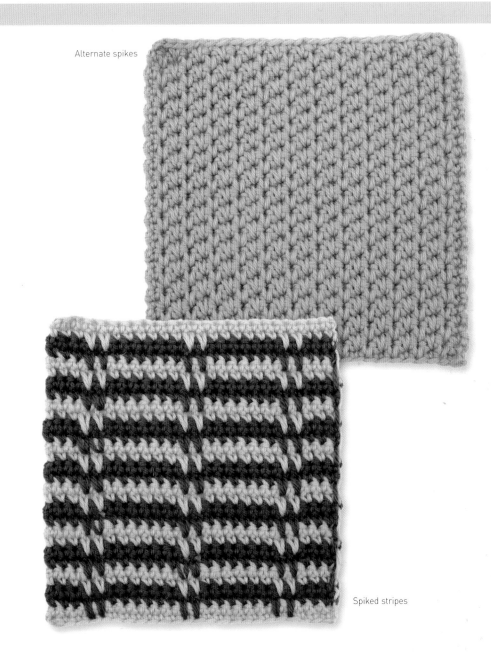

This lovely stitch makes a thick, textured fabric. Worked in one color, the fabric is reversible, so you can choose which side of the work you like best, and use that as the right side.

NOTE: SP = spike stitch made by inserting hook into work one row below next stitch and working a single crochet stitch.

FOUNDATION ROW: 1 sc into 2nd ch from hook, 1 sc into each ch to end, turn.

ROW 1: Ch 1, 1 sc into first sc, * SP, 1 sc into next sc; rep from * to end, turn.

ROW 2: Ch 1, 1 sc into each of first 2 sc, * SP, 1 sc into next sc; rep from * to last sc, 1 sc into last sc, turn.

Rep row 2 for length required.

Alternate spikes

Spiked stripes

RAISED STITCHES

STITCHES MADE WITH THIS TECHNIQUE ARE KNOWN BY SEVERAL DIFFERENT NAMES: RAISED STITCHES, POST STITCHES, OR RELIEF STITCHES. THEY CREATE A HEAVILY TEXTURED SURFACE, MADE BY INSERTING THE HOOK AROUND THE POST (STEM) OF THE STITCHES ON THE PREVIOUS ROW, AND THEN WORKING A DOUBLE CROCHET STITCH. THE HOOK CAN BE INSERTED FROM THE FRONT OR THE BACK OF THE WORK, GIVING A DIFFERENT EFFECT EACH WAY.

Tip

If you are finding it difficult to figure out where to insert your hook, try practicing this technique on a larger scale by using a thick yarn and large hook.

INSERTING THE HOOK

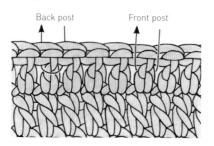

Back post   Front post

When working a front post stitch, insert the hook into the front of the fabric, around the back of the post, and return to the front of the work. When working a back post stitch, insert the hook from the back of the fabric, around the front of the post, and return to the back of the work.

WORKING A RAISED STITCH FROM THE FRONT

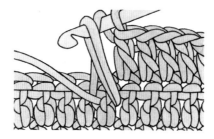

Wrap the yarn over the hook, insert the hook as described above, wrap the yarn over the hook again, and draw up a loop at the front of the work. Complete the double crochet stitch as usual.

WORKING A RAISED STITCH FROM THE BACK

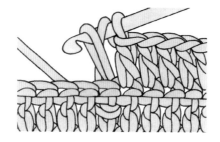

Wrap the yarn over the hook, insert the hook as described above, wrap the yarn over the hook again, and draw up a loop at the back of the work. Complete the double crochet stitch as usual.

Stitch collection

Raised columns

MULTIPLE OF 8 CHAINS PLUS 2

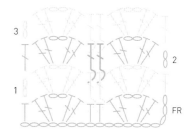

Raised stitches look good when combined with other decorative crochet stitches, particularly those with a flatter surface. Here, vertical rows of raised stitches combine well with simple double crochet shells.

NOTE: FP = raised double crochet stitch worked around the front post (front raised double crochet stitch).
BP = raised double crochet stitch worked around the back post (back raised double crochet stitch).

FOUNDATION ROW: (RS) 2 dc into 6th ch from hook, * ch 2, 2 dc into next ch, sk next 2 chs, 1 hdc into each of next 2 chs, sk next 2 chs, 2 dc into next ch; rep from * to last 3 chs, sk next 2 chs, 1 hdc into last ch, turn.

ROW 1: Ch 2, sk hdc and next 2 dc, * [2 dc, ch 2, 2 dc] into next ch 2 sp, sk next 2 dc, BP around each of next 2 hdc; rep from * ending last rep with 1 dc into 5th of beg skipped ch 5, turn.

ROW 2: Ch 2, sk first 3 dc, * [2 dc, ch 2, 2 dc] into next ch 2 sp, sk next 2 dc, FP around each of next 2 dc; rep from * ending last rep with 1 dc into 2nd of ch 2, turn.

ROW 3: Ch 2, sk first 3 dc, * [2 dc, ch 2, 2 dc] into next ch 2 sp, sk next 2 dc, BP around each of next 2 dc; rep from * ending last rep with 1 dc into 2nd of ch 2, turn.
Rep rows 2 and 3 for length required, ending with a row 3.

Raised columns using double knitting yarn and a standard hook.

Raised columns using medium-weight yarn and an extra large hook.

Basketweave

> ### MULTIPLE OF 8 CHAINS PLUS 4

This heavily worked stitch looks like a woven basket. It is perfect for making pillow covers and thick, warm throws and blankets, but you should be aware that it will use up yarn very quickly.

NOTE: FP = raised double crochet stitch worked around the front post (front raised double crochet stitch).

BP = raised double crochet stitch worked around the back post (back raised double crochet stitch).

FOUNDATION ROW: 1 dc into 4th ch from hook, 1 dc into each ch to end, turn.

ROW 1: Ch 2, sk first dc, * FP around each of next 4 dc, BP around each of next 4 dc; rep from * ending last rep with 1 dc into 3rd of beg skipped ch 3, turn.

ROWS 2–4: Ch 2, sk first dc, * FP around each of next 4 dc, BP around each of next 4 dc; rep from * ending last rep with 1 dc into 2nd of ch 2, turn.

ROWS 5–8: Ch 2, sk first dc, * BP around each of next 4 dc, FP around each of next 4 dc; rep from * ending last rep with 1 dc into 2nd of ch 2, turn.

ROW 9: Ch 2, sk first dc, * FP around each of next 4 dc, BP around each of next 4 dc; rep from * ending last rep with 1 dc into 2nd of ch 2, turn.

Rep rows 2–9 for length required, ending with a row 4.

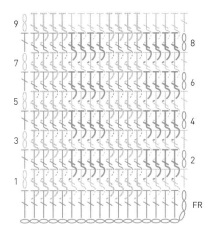

JACQUARD PATTERNS

JACQUARD PATTERNS ARE WORKED IN TWO OR MORE COLORS FROM A CHART, USUALLY IN SINGLE CROCHET. THIS TYPE OF CROCHET CREATES A COLORFUL, STURDY FABRIC WITH A WOVEN LOOK TO IT.

Begin by working the foundation chain in the first color. Calculate the number of chains to make according to the number of times you intend to repeat the pattern, then add one turning chain. On the first row, work the first single crochet stitch into the second chain from the hook, then work the rest of the row in single crochet. Each square represents one stitch. When changing yarns, carry the yarn not in use loosely across the back of the work and pick it up again when it is needed. This is called stranding and it works well when the areas of color are narrow.

WORKING A TWO-COLOR JACQUARD PATTERN

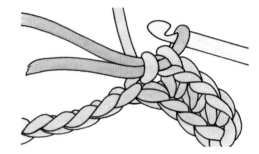

1 Make the required length of foundation chain in yarn A, turn, and begin to work the first row of the chart. When you reach the last stitch worked in yarn A, omit the final stage of the single crochet stitch, leaving two loops on the hook.

2 Join yarn B by drawing a loop of the new color through the two loops on the hook. This completes the last single crochet stitch worked in yarn A. Do not break off yarn A.

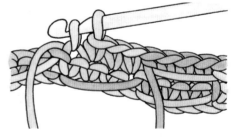

3 Continue to work across the chart in yarn B. When you reach the last stitch worked in yarn B, change back to yarn A by carrying it loosely behind the work. Draw a loop of it through to finish the last stitch worked in yarn B and complete the color change. Continue changing yarns in this way across the row, repeating the pattern as indicated on the chart.

4 At the end of the row, turn and work the chart in the opposite direction from left to right. At the color changes, bring the old color forward and take the new one to the back, ready to complete the stitch partially worked in the old color. Carry the color not in use loosely along the wrong side of the work.

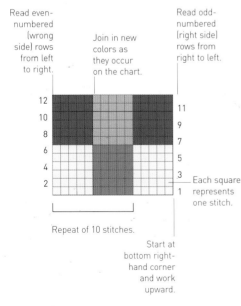

Read even-numbered (wrong side) rows from left to right.

Join in new colors as they occur on the chart.

Read odd-numbered (right side) rows from right to left.

Each square represents one stitch.

Repeat of 10 stitches.

Start at bottom right-hand corner and work upward.

12 10 8 6 4 2
11 9 7 5 3 1

Stitch collection

Jacquard stripes

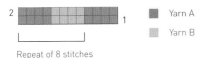

	Yarn A
	Yarn B

Repeat of 8 stitches

Working several repeats of this simple stripe pattern makes a good practice piece. It is important to carry the yarn not in use loosely across the wrong side of the work to avoid it pulling and distorting the pattern.

Jacquard checks

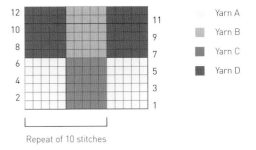

	Yarn A
	Yarn B
	Yarn C
	Yarn D

Repeat of 10 stitches

This checkerboard pattern uses four different yarns, and looks best when four shades of the same color are selected. Choose one light shade, one dark, and two slightly contrasting mid-tones.

KEY TO ABBREVIATIONS AND SYMBOLS pages 150–151

INTARSIA PATTERNS

INTARSIA CROCHET PRODUCES A DESIGN THAT IS VISIBLE ON BOTH SIDES OF THE FABRIC. INTARSIA PATTERNS ARE WORKED IN TWO OR MORE COLORS FROM A CHART.

SEE ALSO

• Jacquard patterns, pages 68–69

The main difference between intarsia and jacquard is that, in intarsia, the color areas are larger and may be irregularly shaped, so colors not in use cannot be carried across the back of the work. Instead, work each color area using a separate ball of yarn. Work the foundation chain in the first color, working the same number of chains as the number of squares across the chart and adding one chain for turning. If you are working a repeating intarsia pattern, calculate the number of chains to make at the start of the project in the same way as for a jacquard pattern.

WORKING AN INTARSIA PATTERN

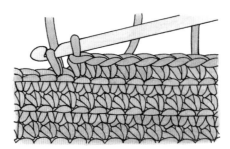

1 Make the required length of foundation chain in yarn A, turn, and work the plain rows at the bottom of the chart in single crochet. Work the first multicolored row, beginning with yarn A. At the color changes, omit the final stage of the stitch before the change, leaving two loops on the hook. Join the next yarn by drawing a loop of the new color through the two loops. This completes the last stitch worked in the first yarn. Continue in this way along the row.

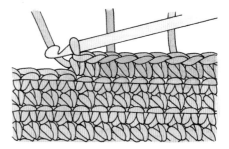

2 When you reach the last color change in the row, where the chart indicates a change back to yarn A, work with another ball of the same yarn, not the one you used to begin the row.

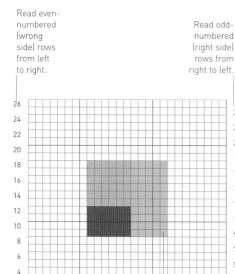

Read even-numbered (wrong side) rows from left to right.

Read odd-numbered (right side) rows from right to left.

Each square represents one stitch.

Join in new colors as they occur on the chart.

Start at bottom right-hand corner and work upward.

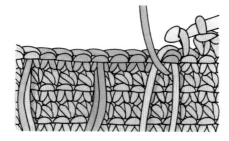

3 At the end of the row, turn and work from the chart in the opposite direction, from left to right. At each color change, bring the old color forward and take the new one to the back, ready to complete the stitch partially worked in the old color. Make sure that you loop the new yarn around the old one on the wrong side of the work to prevent holes.

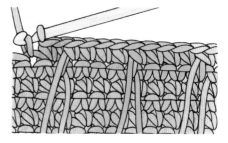

4 At the end of wrong side rows, make sure that all of the yarns are back on the wrong side of the work.

Stitch collection

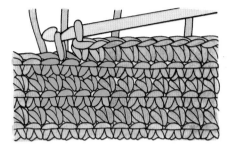

5 When you reach new areas of color farther up the chart, join in the yarns as before, making sure that you work each color change into the last stitch of the previous color.

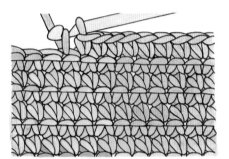

6 When you reach the point in the chart where all the stitches in a row are worked in yarn A, work across all the stitches using the original ball of this color.

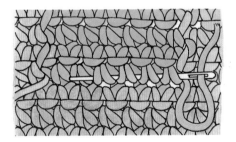

7 Take extra care when dealing with all the yarn ends on a piece of intarsia. Carefully weave each end into an area of crochet worked in the same color so that it will not be visible on the right side.

Intarsia blocks

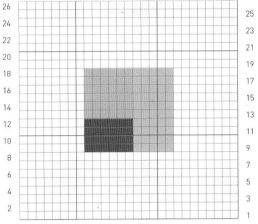

☐ Yarn A
▨ Yarn B
▨ Yarn C
▨ Yarn D

This simple block pattern will give you experience in working intarsia color changes. It is worked in four colors, A, B, C, and D. You can work the chart exactly as it is, or repeat it several times to make a bigger piece of crochet.

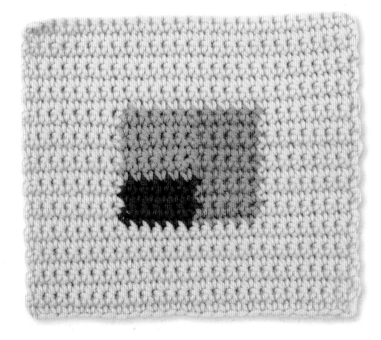

TUBULAR CROCHET

TUBULAR CROCHET IS WORKED IN THE ROUND USING AN ORDINARY CROCHET HOOK. ALTHOUGH THE ROUNDS ARE WORKED AND JOINED IN A SIMILAR WAY TO THOSE USED TO MAKE A CIRCULAR MOTIF, THE EFFECT HERE IS VERY DIFFERENT.

SEE ALSO

• Circular motifs, pages 74–79

This type of crochet forms a cylinder that can be as wide or narrow as you wish. This handy technique means that you can make an item such as a hat in one piece without a seam. Cylinders can also be combined with motifs or flat pieces of crochet to make garments and accessories.

Tubular crochet can be worked in three different ways, but each one begins with a length of chain joined into a ring. You can work rounds of single crochet stitches without making a join; this forms a spiral shape. When using taller stitches such as double crochet, each round is joined to make a seam. If you turn the work at the end of each round, you will produce a straight seam; if you continue working in the same direction on every round, the seam will spiral around the cylinder.

WORKING A SPIRAL CYLINDER IN SINGLE CROCHET

1 Make the required length of chain and join it into a ring with a slip stitch. Turn and work one row of single crochet stitches into the chain. Join the round by working a single crochet into the first stitch of the round.

2 Insert a ring marker into the single crochet stitch just worked to mark the beginning of a new round. Continue working the new round, working a single crochet into each stitch of the previous round.

Single crochet cylinder worked in a spiral.

3 When you reach the marker, do not join the round. Instead, remove the marker and work the marked stitch.

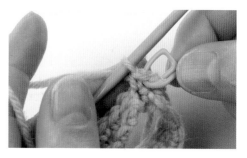

4 Replace the marker in the new stitch to mark the start of the new round. Continue working around and around, moving the marker each time you reach it, until the cylinder is the required length, then fasten off the yarn.

WORKING A DOUBLE CROCHET CYLINDER WITHOUT TURNS

1 Make the required length of chain and join it into a ring with a slip stitch.

2 Work three chains (or the correct number of chains for the stitch you are using) to start the first round.

3 Work one double crochet stitch into each chain until you reach the end of the round.

4 Join the first round by working a slip stitch into the third of the three starting chains.

5 Work the next and subsequent rounds in double crochet stitch, joining each round with a slip stitch as before. When all the rounds have been worked, fasten off the yarn.

Double crochet cylinder worked without turns.

Double crochet cylinder worked with turns.

WORKING A DOUBLE CROCHET CYLINDER WITH TURNS

1 Work the foundation chain and first round of stitches as described in steps 1–4 of making a double crochet cylinder without turns. Work three chains to begin the second round.

2 Turn the cylinder to reverse the direction to begin the second round. You will be working this round from the inside of the cylinder.

3 Work one double crochet stitch into each stitch until you reach the end of the round. Join the round by working a slip stitch into the third of the three turning chains. Turn and work three chains, then work the next round from the outside of the cylinder. Continue in this way, making sure that you turn the work at the beginning of every round.

CIRCULAR MOTIFS

WORKING CROCHET IN FLAT ROUNDS RATHER THAN BACKWARD AND FORWARD IN STRAIGHT ROWS OFFERS A NEW RANGE OF POSSIBILITIES FOR MAKING COLORFUL AND INTRICATE PIECES OF CROCHET CALLED MOTIFS OR MEDALLIONS.

SEE ALSO
- Basic skills and stitches, pages 14–21
- Joining yarns, page 24

A MOTIF WITH MANY USES
Circular motifs are often worked in a variety of yarns and sizes to make items such as coasters and table mats.

Crochet motifs are worked outward from a central ring and the number of stitches on each round increases. Evenly spaced increases result in a flat, circular motif, but when the increases are grouped together to make corners, the resulting motif can be a square, hexagon, or other flat shape. Motifs can be solid, textured, or lacy in appearance. They are joined together using a variety of techniques to make afghans, shawls, and wraps, as well as simply shaped garments.

WORKING IN ROUNDS
The usual way of starting to work a motif is to make a short length of chain and join it into a ring. The ring can be made any size, depending on the pattern instructions, and can leave a small or large hole at the center of the motif.

MAKING A RING OF STITCHES

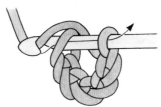

1 Work the number of chains stated in the pattern and join into a ring by working a slip stitch into the first stitch of this chain.

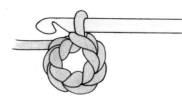

2 Gently tighten the first stitch by pulling the loose yarn end with your left hand. The foundation ring is now complete.

WORKING INTO THE RING

1 After making the foundation ring, you are ready to begin the first round of the pattern. Work the number of starting chains stated in the pattern—three chains are shown here and will count as one double crochet stitch.

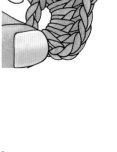

2 Inserting the hook into the space at the center of the ring each time, work the correct number of stitches into the ring as stated in the pattern. Count the stitches at the end of the round to make sure that you have worked the correct number.

3 Join the first and last stitches of the round together by working a slip stitch into the top of the starting chain.

MAKING A YARN RING

This alternative method of making a foundation ring is useful because the yarn end is enclosed in the first round of stitches and will not need weaving in later.

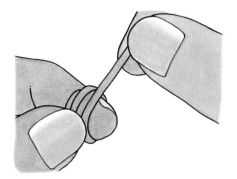

1 Hold the yarn end between the thumb and forefinger of your left hand and wind the yarn several times around the tip of your forefinger.

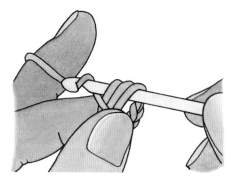

2 Carefully slip the yarn ring off your finger. Inserting the hook into the ring, pull a loop of yarn through and work a single crochet stitch to secure the ring. Work the specified number of starting chains and the first round of pattern into the ring in the usual way.

FASTENING OFF

For a really neat edge on the final round, use this method of sewing the first and last stitches together in preference to using a slip stitch.

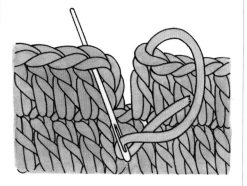

1 Cut the yarn, leaving an end of about 4in (10cm), and draw it through the last stitch. With right side facing, thread the yarn end into a yarn or tapestry needle and take the needle under both loops of the stitch next to the starting chain.

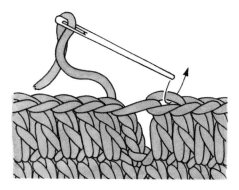

2 Pull the needle through and insert it into the center of the last stitch of the round. On the wrong side, pull the needle through to complete the stitch. Adjust the length of the stitch to close the round, then weave in the end on the wrong side in the usual way.

JOINING ROUND MOTIFS

Circular motifs join less easily than motifs with straight sides because of their curved shape. They look best arranged in rows and sewn together with a few stitches where the curves touch.

Stitch collection

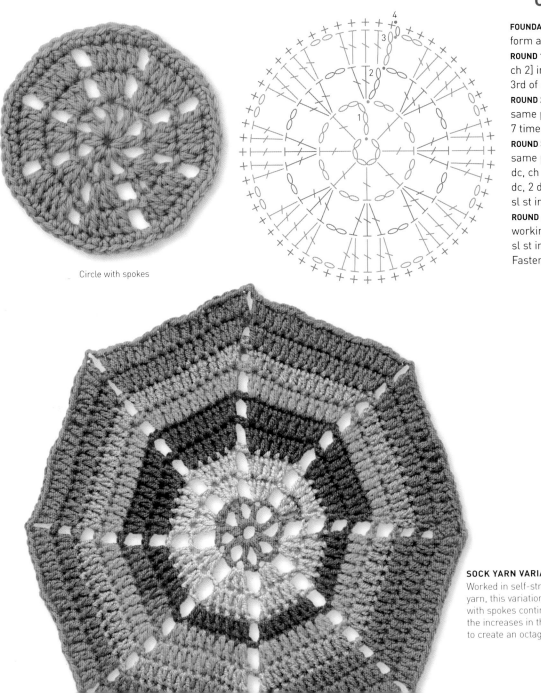

Circle with spokes

Circle with spokes

FOUNDATION RING: Ch 6 and join with sl st to form a ring.

ROUND 1: Ch 5 (counts as 1 dc, ch 2), [1 dc, ch 2] into ring 7 times, join with sl st into 3rd of ch 5. (8 spaced dc)

ROUND 2: Ch 3 (counts as 1 dc), 2 dc into same place, ch 2, [3 dc into next dc, ch 2] 7 times, join with sl st into 3rd of ch 3.

ROUND 3: Ch 3 (counts as 1 dc), 1 dc into same place, 1 dc into next dc, 2 dc into next dc, ch 2, [2 dc into next dc, 1 dc into next dc, 2 dc into next dc, ch 2] 7 times, join with sl st into 3rd of ch 3.

ROUND 4: Ch 1, 1 sc into each dc to end working 2 sc into each ch 2 sp, join with sl st into first sc.
Fasten off yarn.

SOCK YARN VARIATION
Worked in self-striping sock yarn, this variation of the circle with spokes continues to work the increases in the pattern set to create an octagon.

Double crochet circle

FOUNDATION RING: Ch 6 and join with sl st to form a ring.

ROUND 1: Ch 3 (counts as 1 dc), 15 dc into ring, join with sl st into 3rd of ch 3. (16 dc)

ROUND 2: Ch 3 (counts as 1 dc), 1 dc into same place, 2 dc into each dc to end, join with sl st into 3rd of ch 3. (32 dc)

ROUND 3: Ch 3 (counts as 1 dc), 1 dc into same place, * [1 dc into next dc, 2 dc into next dc]; rep from * to last dc, 1 dc into last dc, join with sl st into 3rd of ch 3. (48 dc)

ROUND 4: Ch 3 (counts as 1 dc), 1 dc into same place, * [1 dc into each of next 2 dc, 2 dc into next dc]; rep from * to last 2 dc, 1 dc into each of last 2 dc, join with sl st into 3rd of ch 3. (64 dc)

Fasten off yarn.

This circle can be made larger than shown by working one more double crochet stitch between the increases on each subsequent round.

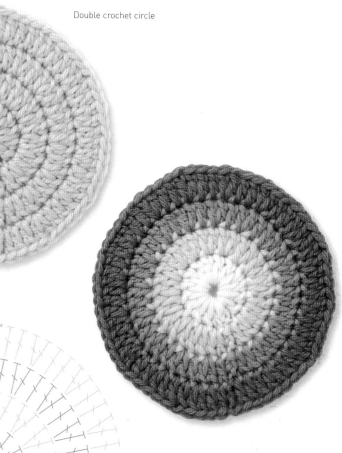

Double crochet circle

STRIPED VARIATION

Work the double crochet circle using a different yarn color on every round. Leave a 4in (10cm) end of yarn at each color change, and weave in the yarn ends on the wrong side when the circle is complete.

KEY TO ABBREVIATIONS AND SYMBOLS **pages 150–151**

Stitch collection

Sunburst circle

YARN: Worked in three colors, A, B, and C.

NOTE: beg CL = beginning cluster made from two double crochet stitches worked together (dc2tog).

CL = cluster made from three double crochet stitches worked together (dc3tog).

FOUNDATION RING: Using yarn A, ch 4 and join with sl st to form a ring.

ROUND 1: Ch 1, 6 sc into ring, join with sl st into first sc.

ROUND 2: Ch 1, 2 sc into each sc to end, join with sl st into first sc. (12 sc)

ROUND 3: Ch 1, 2 sc into each sc to end, join with sl st into first sc. (24 sc)
Break off yarn A and join yarn B to any sc.

ROUND 4: Ch 3 (counts as 1 dc), beg CL into same sc, ch 2, sk next sc, * CL into next sc, ch 2, sk next sc; rep from * 10 times, join with sl st into top of beg CL.
Break off yarn B and join yarn C to any ch 2 sp.

ROUND 5: Ch 3 (counts as 1 dc), beg CL into same sp, ch 3, * CL into next ch 2 sp, ch 3; rep from * 10 times, join with sl st into top of beg CL.

ROUND 6: Ch 3, 2 dc into top of beg CL, 3 dc into next ch 3 sp, * 3 dc into top of next CL, 3 dc into next ch 3 sp; rep from * 10 times, join with sl st into 3rd of ch 3.
Fasten off yarn.

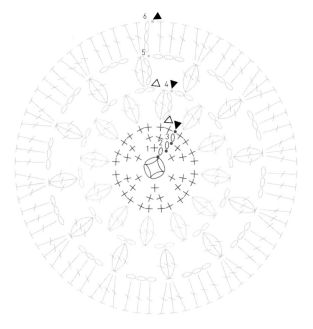

Cluster circle

NOTE: beg CL = beginning cluster made from three double crochet stitches worked together (dc3tog).

CL = cluster made from four double crochet stitches worked together (dc4tog).

FOUNDATION RING: Ch 6 and join with sl st to form a ring.

ROUND 1: Ch 1, 12 sc into ring, join with sl st into first sc.

ROUND 2: Ch 4 (counts as 1 dc, ch 1), * 1 dc into next sc, ch 1; rep from * 10 times, join with sl st into 3rd of ch 4. (12 spaced dc)

ROUND 3: Sl st into next ch 1 sp, ch 3 (counts as 1 dc), beg CL into same sp, ch 3, * CL into next ch 1 sp, ch 3; rep from * 10 times, join with sl st into top of beg CL. (12 clusters)

ROUND 4: Sl st into next ch 3 sp, ch 3 (counts as 1 dc), beg CL into same sp, * ch 2, 1 dc into top of next CL, ch 2, ** CL into next ch 3 sp; rep from * 10 times and from * to ** once again, join with sl st into top of beg CL.

ROUND 5: Ch 1, 3 sc into each ch 2 sp to end, join with sl st into first sc.
Fasten off yarn.

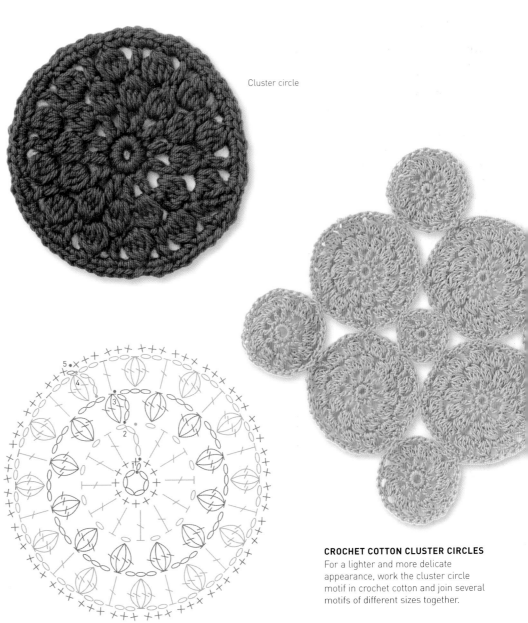

Cluster circle

CROCHET COTTON CLUSTER CIRCLES
For a lighter and more delicate appearance, work the cluster circle motif in crochet cotton and join several motifs of different sizes together.

KEY TO ABBREVIATIONS AND SYMBOLS pages 150–151

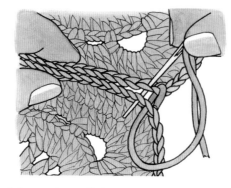

SQUARE MOTIFS

SQUARE MOTIFS ARE WORKED IN A SIMILAR WAY TO CIRCULAR MOTIFS, STARTING AT THE CENTER WITH A FOUNDATION RING AND WORKING OUTWARD IN ROUNDS.

SEE ALSO
- Basic skills and stitches, pages 14–21
- Circular motifs, pages 74–79

Extra stitches or chains are worked at regular intervals on some of the rounds to form corners. Some motifs, such as the granny square (see page 84), begin with a small circle at the center. Others, such as the circle in a square (see page 83), have several rounds worked before the corners are made.

JOINING MOTIFS WITH A NEEDLE

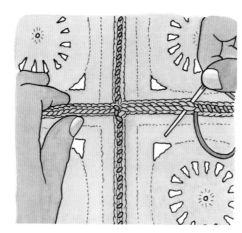

1 Lay out the motifs in the correct order, with right sides facing upward. Using a yarn or tapestry needle and working in horizontal rows, stitch the motifs together, beginning with the top row of motifs. Begin stitching at the right-hand edge of the first two motifs, sewing into the back loops of corresponding stitches.

JOINING SQUARE MOTIFS
Square motifs can be stitched together or joined with rows of slip stitches or single crochet. For the neatest join, work the stitches through the back loops of the crochet. To make a stronger but more visible join, work the stitches through both loops.

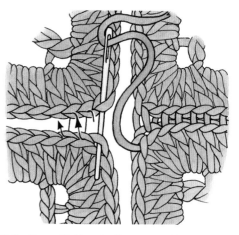

2 Continue stitching the first two motifs together, making sure that you join only the back loops of each edge together, until you reach the left-hand corner. Align the next two motifs, carry the yarn firmly across, and join them together in the same way. For extra strength, you can work two stitches into the corner loops before and after carrying the yarn across. Continue joining motifs along the row, then secure the yarn ends carefully at the beginning and end of the stitching. Repeat until all the horizontal edges of the motifs are joined.

3 Turn the crochet so that the unstitched (vertical) edges of the motifs are now horizontal. Working in the same way as before, join the remaining edges together with horizontal rows of stitching. When working the corners, take the needle under the stitch made on the previous row of stitching.

Tip
When joining two differently colored squares by stitching them together, use a yarn that matches one of the squares so that the stitches are less noticeable.

JOINING MOTIFS WITH SLIP STITCH

Joining motif edges by slip stitching them together with a crochet hook makes a firm seam with an attractive ridge on the right side. To add interest, use a contrasting yarn color to work the slip stitch rows.

JOINING MOTIFS WITH SINGLE CROCHET

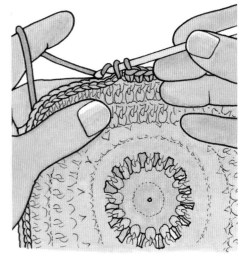

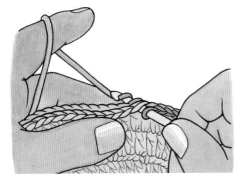

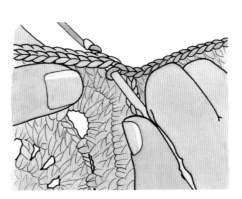

1 Lay out the motifs in the correct order. Working all the horizontal seams first, place the first two motifs together, wrong sides facing, and work a row of slip stitch through both loops of each motif.

2 When you reach the corner, align the next two motifs, carry the yarn firmly across, and join them together in the same way. Continue joining motifs along the row, keeping your tension even. Secure the yarn ends carefully, then repeat until all the horizontal edges of the motifs are joined.

Single crochet can also be used to join edges together, and it makes a strong but rather bulky, thick seam. Work as for joining with slip stitch, but place the motifs right sides together and work rows of single crochet through both loops of the crochet edge.

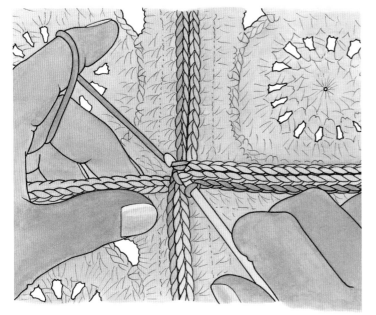

3 Turn the work so that the remaining (vertical) edges of the motifs are now horizontal. Working in the same way as before, join the remaining edges together with horizontal rows of slip stitch. When working the corners, carry the yarn firmly across the ridge.

Tip

If you are finding it difficult to insert your hook through the edges of the squares when joining motifs, use a slightly smaller hook or one that has a more pointed tip.

Stitch collection

Croydon square

YARN: Worked in three colors, A, B, and C.
NOTE: beg CL = beginning cluster made from two double crochet stitches worked together (dc2tog).
CL = cluster made from three double crochet stitches worked together (dc3tog).
FOUNDATION RING: Using yarn A, ch 4 and join with sl st to form a ring.
ROUND 1: Ch 4 (counts as 1 dc, ch 1), [1 dc into ring, ch 1] 11 times, join with sl st into 3rd of ch 4. (12 spaced dc)
ROUND 2: Ch 3 (counts as 1 dc), beg CL into same sp, [ch 3, CL into next ch 1 sp] 11 times, ch 3, join with sl st into top of beg CL.
ROUND 3: Sl st into center st of next ch 3 sp, ch 1, 1 sc into same sp, [ch 5, 1 sc into next ch 3 sp] 11 times, ch 5, join with sl st into first sc.
Break off yarn A and join yarn B to center st of any ch 5 sp.
ROUND 4: Ch 3 (counts as 1 dc), 4 dc into same sp, * ch 1, 1 sc into next ch 5 sp, ch 5, 1 sc into next ch 5 sp, ch 1, ** [5 dc, ch 3, 5 dc] into next ch 5 sp; rep from * twice and from * to ** once again, 5 dc into next ch 5 sp, ch 3, join with sl st into 3rd of ch 3.
Break off yarn B and join yarn C to any ch 3 sp.
ROUND 5: Ch 3 (counts as 1 dc), [1 dc, ch 2, 2 dc] into same sp, * 1 dc into each of next 4 dc, ch 4, 1 sc into next ch 5 sp, ch 4, sk next dc, 1 dc into each of next 4 dc, ** [2 dc, ch 2, 2 dc] into next ch 3 sp; rep from * twice and from * to ** once again, join with sl st into 3rd of ch 3.

ROUND 6: Sl st into next dc and next ch 2 sp, ch 3 (counts as 1 dc), [1 dc, ch 2, 2 dc] into same sp, * 1 dc into each of next 4 dc, [ch 4, 1 dc into next ch 4 sp] twice, ch 4, sk next 2 dc, 1 dc into each of next 4 dc, ** [2 dc, ch 2, 2 dc] into next ch 2 sp; rep from * twice and from * to ** once again, join with sl st into 3rd of ch 3.
ROUND 7: Ch 1, 1 sc into same place, 1 sc into each dc to end working 4 sc into each ch 4 sp along sides and 3 sc into each ch 2 corner sp, join with sl st into first sc.
Fasten off yarn.

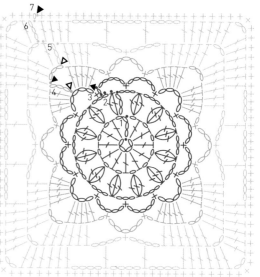

Circle in a square

FOUNDATION RING: Ch 6 and join with sl st to form a ring.

ROUND 1: Ch 3 (counts as 1 dc), work 15 dc into ring, join with sl st into 3rd of ch 3. (16 dc)

ROUND 2: Ch 5 (counts as 1 dc, ch 2), [1 dc into next dc, ch 2] 15 times, join with sl st into 3rd of ch 5.

ROUND 3: Ch 3, 2 dc into ch 2 sp, ch 1, [3 dc, ch 1] into each ch 2 sp to end, join with sl st into 3rd of ch 3.

ROUND 4: * [Ch 3, 1 sc into next ch 1 sp] 3 times, ch 6 (corner sp made), 1 sc into next ch 1 sp; rep from * to end, join with sl st into first of ch 3.

ROUND 5: Ch 3, 2 dc into first ch 3 sp, 3 dc into each of next two ch 3 sps, * [5 dc, ch 2, 5 dc] into corner sp, ** 3 dc into each of next three ch 3 sps; rep from * twice and from * to ** once again, join with sl st into 3rd of ch 3.

ROUND 6: Ch 3, 1 dc into each dc to end working [1 dc, 1 tr, 1 dc] into each ch 2 corner sp, join with sl st into 3rd of ch 3.

Fasten off yarn.

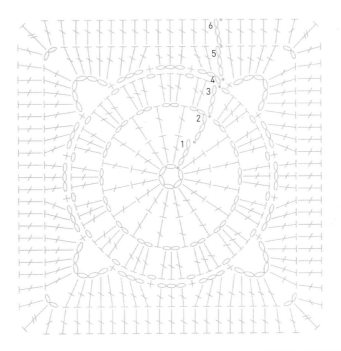

KEY TO ABBREVIATIONS AND SYMBOLS **pages 150–151**

Stitch collection

Granny square

YARN: Worked in four colors, A, B, C, and D.

FOUNDATION RING: Using yarn A, ch 6 and join with sl st to form a ring.

ROUND 1: Ch 3 (counts as 1 dc), 2 dc into ring, ch 3, * 3 dc into ring, ch 3; rep from * twice, join with sl st into 3rd of ch 3.
Break off yarn A and join yarn B to any ch 3 sp.

ROUND 2: Ch 3 (counts as 1 dc), [2 dc, ch 3, 3 dc] into same sp (corner made), * ch 1, [3 dc, ch 3, 3 dc] into next ch 3 sp; rep from * twice, ch 1, join with sl st into 3rd of ch 3.
Break off yarn B and join yarn C to any ch 3 corner sp.

ROUND 3: Ch 3 (counts as 1 dc), [2 dc, ch 3, 3 dc] into same sp, * ch 1, 3 dc into next ch 1 sp, ch 1, ** [3 dc, ch 3, 3 dc] into next ch 3 corner sp; rep from * twice and from * to ** once again, join with sl st into 3rd of ch 3.
Break off yarn C and join yarn D to any ch 3 corner sp.

ROUND 4: Ch 3 (counts as 1 dc), [2 dc, ch 3, 3 dc] into same sp, * [ch 1, 3 dc] into each ch 1 sp along side of square, ch 1, ** [3 dc, ch 3, 3 dc] into next ch 3 corner sp; rep from * twice and from * to ** once again, join with sl st into 3rd of ch 3.
Break off yarn D and join yarn A to any ch 3 corner sp.

ROUND 5: Ch 3 (counts as 1 dc), [2 dc, ch 3, 3 dc] into same sp, * [ch 1, 3 dc] into each ch 1 sp along side of square, ch 1, ** [3 dc, ch 3, 3 dc] into next ch 3 corner sp; rep from * twice and from * to ** once again, join with sl st into 3rd of ch 3.

ROUND 6: Sl st into next ch 3 corner sp, ch 3 (counts as 1 dc), [2 dc, ch 3, 3 dc] into same sp, * [ch 1, 3 dc] into each ch 1 sp along side of square, ch 1, ** [3 dc, ch 3, 3 dc] into next ch 3 corner sp; rep from * twice and from * to ** once again, join with sl st into 3rd of ch 3.
Fasten off yarn.

KEY TO ABBREVIATIONS AND SYMBOLS **pages 150–151**

HEXAGON MOTIFS

HEXAGON MOTIFS ARE WORKED IN A SIMILAR WAY TO CIRCULAR AND SQUARE MOTIFS, BUT THEY NEED DIFFERENT SEQUENCES OF INCREASES TO MAKE SIX CORNERS. HEXAGON MOTIFS WITH A SOLIDLY CROCHETED LAST ROUND CAN BE STITCHED OR CROCHETED TOGETHER TO MAKE LARGE PIECES OF CROCHET SUCH AS AFGHANS, THROWS, AND SHAWLS IN THE SAME WAY AS SQUARE MOTIFS.

SEE ALSO

- Basic skills and stitches, pages 14–21
- Circular motifs, pages 74–79
- Square motifs, pages 80–84

The centers of hexagon motifs may have a circular or hexagonal shape, depending on the pattern. When working a motif with a hexagonal center, remember that you will be working six corners rather than the four needed for a square, so you need to work the foundation ring fairly loosely in order to make sure that the finished hexagon will lie flat.

BEGINNING WITH A HEXAGONAL CENTER

1 Work the foundation ring, then work six groups of stitches separated by chain spaces as indicated in the pattern to make a hexagon shape. Join the round with a slip stitch in the usual way.

2 On the second round, work two groups of stitches separated by a chain space into each of the chain spaces on the previous round to continue making a hexagon shape. Work additional rows as indicated in the pattern.

You can join hexagons into long strips and then join the strips together, or simply lay out the pieces in the required arrangement and join the edges that touch with separate seams. Pay special attention to securing the yarn ends neatly at the beginning and end of each seam. When joining motifs that have a lacy last round, such as the classic hexagon (see page 87), you can crochet these together as you work.

BEGINNING WITH A CIRCULAR CENTER

1 Work the foundation ring, then work the number of stitches indicated in the pattern. The stitches form a circle, and they may be solidly worked or separated by a single chain space. Join the round with a slip stitch in the usual way.

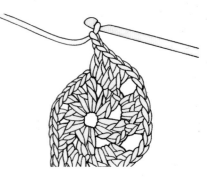

2 On the second round, work groups of stitches separated by chain spaces into the previous round. This creates a hexagon shape in which the corners are formed by chain spaces rather than by groups of stitches. The chain spaces act as a foundation for corners worked on the next and subsequent rounds.

JOINING HEXAGONS AS YOU WORK

To begin, work one complete motif, then join the edges of additional motifs to the original one as you work the final rounds.

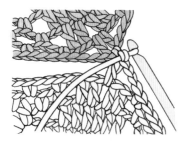

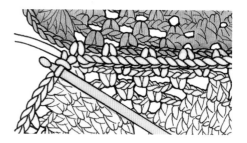

1 Work the second motif until you reach the last round. Work in pattern along the first side, then work the first double crochet stitch of the corner group. Align the edges of both motifs and join by working a single crochet stitch into the chain space of the corner on the first hexagon.

2 Return to the second hexagon and work a double crochet stitch into it to complete the corner.

3 Continue working around the second hexagon, joining the chain spaces of each hexagon together by working one chain, one single crochet into the opposite chain space, and one chain until you reach the next corner. At the corner, work the first double crochet stitch of the pattern, then one single crochet stitch into the chain space of the first hexagon.

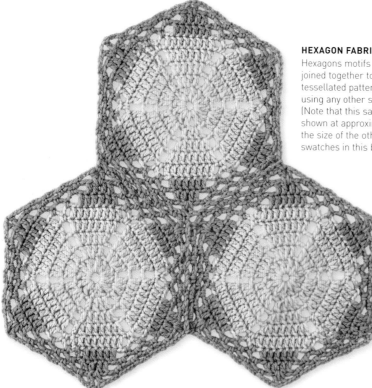

HEXAGON FABRIC

Hexagons motifs can be joined together to create tessellated patterns without using any other shapes. (Note that this sample is shown at approximately half the size of the other sample swatches in this book.)

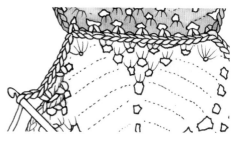

4 Work one double crochet stitch to complete the corner, then work the remainder of the last round as instructed in the pattern. Fasten off the yarn. Join other hexagons to the first two in the same way, joining one, two, or more edges as required.

Tip

You can join the first few hexagons to make a strip and use this as a base for attaching the remaining motifs if you are making a rectangular piece, or begin with one motif and let your piece grow outward from the center.

Stitch collection

Classic hexagon

YARN: Worked in three colors, A, B, and C.

FOUNDATION RING: Using yarn A, ch 6 and join with sl st to form a ring.

ROUND 1: Ch 4 (counts as 1 dc, ch 1), [1 dc into ring, ch 1] 11 times, join with sl st into 3rd of ch 4. (12 spaced dc)

ROUND 2: Ch 3 (counts as 1 dc), 2 dc into next ch 1 sp, 1 dc into next dc, ch 2, * 1 dc into next dc, 2 dc into next ch 1 sp, 1 dc into next dc, ch 2; rep from * 4 times, join with sl st into 3rd of ch 3.

ROUND 3: Ch 3, 1 dc into same place, 1 dc into each of next 2 dc, 2 dc into next dc, ch 2, * 2 dc into next dc, 1 dc into each of next 2 dc, 2 dc into next dc, ch 2; rep from * 4 times, join with sl st into 3rd of ch 3. Break off yarn A and join yarn B.

ROUND 4: Ch 3, 1 dc into same place, 1 dc into each of next 4 dc, 2 dc into next dc, ch 2, * 2 dc into next dc, 1 dc into each of next 4 dc, 2 dc into next dc, ch 2; rep from * 4 times, join with sl st into 3rd of ch 3.

ROUND 5: Ch 3, 1 dc into each of next 7 dc, * ch 3, 1 sc into next ch 2 sp, ch 3, 1 dc into each of next 8 dc; rep from * 4 times, ch 3, 1 sc into next ch 2 sp, ch 3, join with sl st into 3rd of ch 3.
Break off yarn B and join yarn C into top of next dc.

ROUND 6: Ch 3, 1 dc into each of next 5 dc, * ch 3, [1 sc into next ch 3 sp, ch 3] twice, sk next dc, 1 dc into each of next 6 dc; rep from * 4 times, ch 3, [1 sc into next ch 3 sp, ch 3] twice, join with sl st into 3rd of ch 3.

ROUND 7: Sl st into next dc, ch 3, 1 dc into each of next 3 dc, * ch 3, [1 sc into next ch 3 sp, ch 3] 3 times, sk next dc, 1 dc into each of next 4 dc; rep from * 4 times, ch 3, [1 sc into next ch 3 sp, ch 3] 3 times, join with sl st into 3rd of ch 3.

ROUND 8: Sl st between 2nd and 3rd dc of group, ch 4 (counts as 1 dc, ch 1), 1 dc into same place, * ch 3, [1 sc into next ch 3 sp, ch 3] 4 times, [1 dc, ch 1, 1 dc] between 2nd and 3rd dc of group; rep from * 4 times, ch 3, [1 sc into ch 3 sp, ch 3] 4 times, join with sl st into 3rd of ch 4.
Fasten off yarn.

Stitch collection

Wheel hexagon

FOUNDATION RING: Ch 6 and join with sl st to form a ring.

ROUND 1: Ch 6 (counts as 1 tr, ch 2), 1 tr into ring, * ch 2, 1 tr into ring; rep from * 9 times, ch 2, join with sl st into 4th of ch 6. (12 spaced tr)

ROUND 2: Sl st into next ch 2 sp, ch 3 (counts as 1 dc), [1 dc, ch 2, 2 dc] into same ch 2 sp as sl st, * 3 dc into next ch 2 sp, [2 dc, ch 2, 2 dc] into next ch 2 sp; rep from * 4 times, 3 dc into next ch 2 sp, join with sl st into 3rd of ch 3.

ROUND 3: Ch 3 (counts as 1 dc), 1 dc into next dc, * [2 dc, ch 3, 2 dc] into next ch 2 sp, 1 dc into each of next 7 dc; rep from * 4 times, [2 dc, ch 3, 2 dc] into next ch 2 sp, 1 dc into each of next 5 dc, join with sl st into 3rd of ch 3.

ROUND 4: Ch 3 (counts as 1 dc), 1 dc into each of next 3 dc, * 3 dc into next ch 3 sp, 1 dc into each of next 11 dc; rep from * 4 times, 3 dc into next ch 3 sp, 1 dc into each of next 7 dc, join with sl st into 3rd of ch 3.

Fasten off yarn.

SMALL WHEEL HEXAGON

You can often reduce the size of a motif by simply omitting the final round. To make this small wheel hexagon, omit round 4 and work 2 dc, ch 1, 2 dc into the corner spaces on round 3 (instead of 2 dc, ch 3, 2 dc). This sample has been worked in worsted-weight yarn (rather than double knitting) to give a slightly bulkier appearance, despite the smaller size.

Wheel hexagon

Granny hexagon

YARN: Worked in three colors, A, B, and C.

FOUNDATION RING: Using yarn A, ch 8 and join with sl st to form a ring.

ROUND 1: Ch 3 (counts as 1 dc), 2 dc into ring, ch 3, * 3 dc into ring, ch 3; rep from * 4 times, join with sl st into 3rd of ch 3. Break off yarn A and join yarn B to any ch 3 sp.

ROUND 2: Ch 3 (counts as 1 dc), [2 dc, ch 3, 3 dc] into same sp (corner made), * ch 1, [3 dc, ch 3, 3 dc] into next ch 3 sp (corner made); rep from * 4 times, ch 1, join with sl st into 3rd of ch 3. Break off yarn B and join yarn C to any corner sp.

ROUND 3: Ch 3, [2 dc, ch 3, 3 dc] into same sp, * ch 1, 3 dc into next ch 1 sp, ch 1, [3 dc, ch 3, 3 dc] into next corner sp; rep from * 4 times, ch 1, 3 dc into next ch 1 sp, ch 1, join with sl st into 3rd of ch 3. Break off yarn C and join yarn B to any corner sp.

ROUND 4: Ch 3, [2 dc, ch 3, 3 dc] into same sp, * [ch 1, 3 dc into each ch 1 sp] along side of hexagon, ch 1, [3 dc, ch 3, 3 dc] into next corner sp; rep from * 4 times, [ch 1, 3 dc into each ch 1 sp] along side of hexagon, ch 1, join with sl st into 3rd of ch 3. Break off yarn B and join yarn A to any corner sp.

ROUND 5: Ch 3, [2 dc, ch 3, 3 dc] into same sp, * [ch 1, 3 dc into each ch 1 sp] along side of hexagon, ch 1, [3 dc, ch 3, 3 dc] into next corner sp; rep from * 4 times, [ch 1, 3 dc into each ch 1 sp] along side of hexagon, ch 1, join with sl st into 3rd of ch 3.

ROUND 6: Ch 1, 1 sc into each dc to end working 1 sc into each ch 1 sp along sides of hexagon and 3 sc into each ch 3 corner sp, join with sl st into first sc. Fasten off yarn.

KEY TO ABBREVIATIONS AND SYMBOLS **pages 150–151**

TUNISIAN CROCHET

OFTEN REFERRED TO AS AFGHAN STITCH, TUNISIAN CROCHET COMBINES THE TECHNIQUES OF BOTH CROCHET AND KNITTING TO PRODUCE A STRONG, ELASTIC FABRIC.

SEE ALSO

• Basic skills and stitches, pages 14–21

Tunisian crochet hooks look like long knitting needles with a hook at one end, and they are available in a range of sizes and lengths. The length of the hook determines how wide the crochet fabric can be. Flexible hooks are also available. These consist of a short hooked needle joined to a length of flexible cord with a stopper at the end. Flexible hooks come in longer lengths than ordinary Tunisian hooks, and enable you to work wider pieces of crochet. Yarn and hook are held in the same way as for ordinary crochet.

PLAIN TUNISIAN CROCHET
This basic Tunisian crochet stitch pattern can be adapted using common knitting techniques such as intarsia and cabling.

WORKING PLAIN TUNISIAN STITCH

Tunisian crochet fabric is made on a foundation chain, and each row is worked in two stages. In the first stage, the loop row, a series of loops are made onto the needle, then on the return row the loops are worked off the needle in pairs without turning the work. Plain Tunisian is the simplest technique, but variations can be made by inserting the hook in different positions, and changing how the loops are worked.

1 BEGIN FIRST LOOP ROW: After making a foundation chain in the usual way, insert the hook under the back loop of the second chain from the hook, wrap the yarn over the hook, and draw a loop through the chain so that you have two loops on the hook.

2 Insert the hook under the back loop of the third chain from the hook, wrap the yarn over the hook, and draw a loop through so that you have three loops on the hook.

3 Repeat along the row until you have made a loop from each chain and have a row of loops on the hook. Do not turn the work.

4 BEGIN FIRST RETURN ROW: Wrap the yarn over the hook and draw it through the first loop on the hook. Wrap the yarn over the hook again and draw it through the next two loops on the hook. Continue working from left to right, working off two loops at a time until only one loop remains on the hook.

5 BEGIN SECOND LOOP ROW: To work the second loop row, skip the first vertical bar and insert the hook from right to left under the next vertical bar. Wrap the yarn over the hook and draw it through to make a loop on the hook so that you have two loops on the hook.

6 Insert the hook under the next vertical bar, wrap the yarn over the hook, and draw a loop through so that you have three loops on the hook. Repeat along the row until you have a row of loops on the hook. Do not turn the work.

7 BEGIN SECOND RETURN ROW: To work the return row, wrap the yarn over the hook and draw it through the first loop on the hook, then work off the row of loops in the same way as step 4, leaving one loop on the hook at the end of the row. Repeat from step 5 for length required, ending with a return row.

TUNISIAN CROCHET HOOK
Like knitting, the width of your Tunisian crochet is determined by the length of the hook.

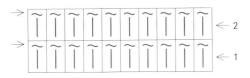

PLAIN TUNISIAN CROCHET CHART
The symbol in each block of this chart indicates that you should work one plain Tunisian crochet stitch.

FINISHING THE TOP EDGE OF TUNISIAN CROCHET

After working a piece of Tunisian crochet, finish off the top edge with a row of single crochet stitches to neaten and strengthen the edge.

1 Wrap the yarn over the hook and draw it through the loop on the hook to make a turning chain.

2 Insert the hook from right to left under the second vertical bar, wrap the yarn over the hook, and draw a loop through so that you have two loops on the hook.

3 Wrap the yarn over the hook again and draw it through both loops on the hook to complete the single crochet stitch.

4 Work a single crochet stitch under each vertical bar of the row, then fasten off the yarn.

Stitch collection

Tunisian knit stitch

ANY NUMBER OF CHAINS PLUS 1

This variation of plain Tunisian crochet looks like knitted stockinette stitch on the right side, but the fabric is thicker and more substantial than stockinette stitch. You may find that you need to use a larger hook when working this stitch.

ROW 1: (LOOP ROW) Insert hook into 2nd ch from hook, yo, draw lp through, * [insert hook into next ch, yo, draw lp through]; rep from * to end, leaving all lps on hook. Do not turn.

ROW 1: (RETURN ROW) Yo, draw through one lp on hook, * [yo, draw through 2 lps on hook]; rep from * to end, leaving last lp on hook.

ROW 2: (LOOP ROW) Sk first vertical bar, insert hook from front to back through next vertical bar, yo, draw lp through, * [insert hook from front to back through next vertical bar, yo, draw lp through]; rep from * to end, leaving all lps on hook. Do not turn.

ROW 2: (RETURN ROW) Yo, draw through one lp on hook, * [yo, draw through 2 lps on hook]; rep from * to end, leaving last lp on hook.

Rep row 2 for length required, ending with return row.

To finish the top edge, work as shown in the step-by-step sequence on the left, but insert the hook from front to back through each vertical bar.

Fasten off yarn.

Tunisian mesh stitch

ANY NUMBER OF CHAINS PLUS 1

This variation makes a lovely, lacy fabric with good drape, perfect for making a baby blanket or shawl.

ROW 1: (LOOP ROW) Insert hook into 3rd ch from hook, yo, draw lp through, ch 1, * [insert hook into next ch, yo, draw lp through, ch 1]; rep from * to end, leaving all lps on hook. Do not turn.

ROW 1: (RETURN ROW) Yo, draw through one lp on hook, * [yo, draw through 2 lps on hook]; rep from * to end, leaving last lp on hook.

ROW 2: (LOOP ROW) Ch 1, sk first vertical bar, * [insert hook under horizontal bar slightly above and behind next vertical bar, yo, draw lp through, ch 1]; rep from * to end, leaving all lps on hook. Do not turn.

ROW 2: (RETURN ROW) Yo, draw through one lp on hook, * [yo, draw through 2 lps on hook]; rep from * to end, leaving last lp on hook.

Rep row 2 for length required, ending with a return row.

To finish the top edge, work as shown in the step-by-step sequence opposite, but insert the hook under the horizontal bar slightly above and behind the next vertical bar. Fasten off yarn.

Tunisian knit stitch

Tunisian mesh stitch

KEY TO ABBREVIATIONS AND SYMBOLS **pages 150–151**

BROOMSTICK CROCHET

BROOMSTICK CROCHET IS WORKED WITH AN ORDINARY CROCHET HOOK AND A LARGE KNITTING NEEDLE, AND MAKES A SOFT, VERY LACY FABRIC.

SEE ALSO
• Basic skills and stitches, pages 14–21

The length of the knitting needle determines the width of the crochet fabric, so you may need to make several strips and sew them together to get the desired width. This technique is used to make shawls, scarves, wraps, and blankets, and it looks good worked in a smooth woolen yarn or a soft mohair.

WHICH SIDE TO USE
Use either the smooth side (above) or the ridged side (left) as the right side of your broomstick crochet fabric.

WORKING BROOMSTICK CROCHET
Each row of broomstick crochet is worked in two stages. In the first stage, the loop row, a series of loops is worked and transferred onto the knitting needle. On the return row, all the loops are slipped off the needle, then crocheted together to make groups. For the beginner, it is best to make a two-row foundation as shown below, but the more experienced crocheter may be able to work the first row directly into a foundation chain.

1 Make a foundation chain to the width required, making sure that you have a multiple of five stitches plus turning chain, then turn and work a row of single crochet into the chain.

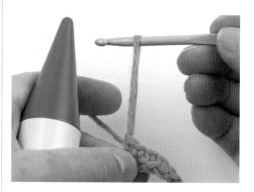

2 **BEGIN LOOP ROW:** Hold the knitting needle securely under your left arm, extend the loop already on the crochet hook, and slip it over the needle.

3 Insert the hook into the second stitch, wrap the yarn over the hook and draw a loop through, then extend the loop and slip it onto the needle.

4 Draw a loop through each stitch of the foundation row in this way to complete the loop row. Check that the number of loops is a multiple of five.

5 BEGIN RETURN ROW: Slip all the loops off the needle and hold the work in your left hand. Insert the hook from right to left through the first five loops.

6 Wrap the yarn over the hook, draw a loop through the center of the five-loop group, and make one chain.

7 Work five single crochet stitches through the center of the loops. Continue along the row of loops in this way, grouping five loops together and working five single crochet stitches through the center of each group of loops to complete the first return row.

8 To work the next loop row, do not turn the work. Extend the first loop over the needle as before, and repeat the loop row as above. Continue working alternate loop and return rows until the fabric is the required length, ending with a return row.

Tip

You may find that broomstick crochet is rather fiddly to work at first, especially when working the loop rows. Gripping the knitting needle between your knees instead of holding it under your arm can make handling the needle easier.

HAIRPIN CROCHET

HAIRPIN CROCHET (ALSO CALLED HAIRPIN LACE AND HAIRPIN BRAID) IS WORKED WITH AN ORDINARY CROCHET HOOK AND A SPECIAL HAIRPIN TOOL. THE TECHNIQUE MAKES STRIPS OF VERY LACY CROCHET THAT ARE OFTEN USED TO DECORATE THE EDGES OF ORDINARY CROCHET.

Hairpin tools are adjustable, so you can make different widths of crochet. The metal pins are held in position by plastic clips or bars at the top and bottom, and the pins can be placed close together to make a narrow strip or moved farther apart to make a wide strip.

A series of loops are made between the two pins using the yarn and the crochet hook until the tool is full of loops. At this point, the loops are taken off the pins, leaving the final few loops on the pins so that work can continue. When the strip reaches the desired length, all the loops are taken off the tool. You can use the hairpin crochet exactly as it comes off the tool, or you can work a row of single crochet stitches along each looped edge if you prefer.

Tip

If you find it difficult to keep the work centered between the pins, secure the yarn end to the bottom clip of the tool with a piece of masking tape after you have centered the knot in step 2.

HAIRPIN CROCHET TOOL
Hairpin crochet tools are adjustable.

HAIRPIN CROCHET STRIP
Strips of hairpin crochet can be joined together to make a fabric.

WORKING HAIRPIN LACE

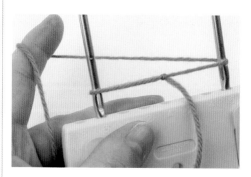

1 Arrange the pins in the bottom clip of the hairpin tool so that the pins are the required distance apart. Make a slip knot in the yarn and loop it over the left-hand pin.

2 Ease the knot across so that it lies in the center between the pins. Take the yarn back around the right-hand pin, tensioning it with your fingers as if you were working ordinary crochet.

3 Insert the crochet hook into the loop on the left-hand pin, wrap the yarn over the hook, and draw it through the loop.

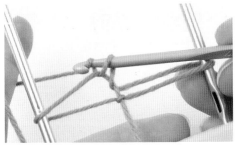

4 Wrap the yarn over the hook again and draw it through the loop on the hook to secure the yarn.

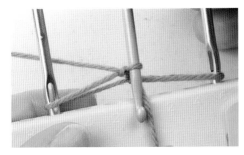

5 Holding the hook vertically, turn the hairpin tool 180 degrees clockwise to make a half turn. The yarn is now wound around the right-hand pin and the other side of the clip is facing you.

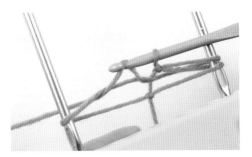

6 Insert the hook under the front loop on the left-hand pin, pick up the yarn at the back of the tool, and draw a loop of yarn through so that there are two loops on the hook.

7 Wrap the yarn over the hook and draw it through the two loops on the hook to make a single crochet stitch.

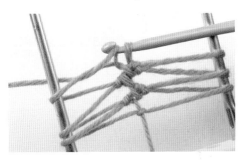

8 Repeat steps 5, 6, and 7 until the hairpin tool is filled with braid, remembering to turn the tool clockwise each time.

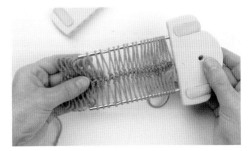

9 When the tool is full, put the top clip onto the pins, remove the lower clip, and slide the crochet strip downward, leaving the last few loops on the pins.

10 Reinsert the lower clip, remove the top clip, and continue working the strip as before. When the strip is the required length, pull the yarn end through the last stitch with the hook, and slide the strip off the pins.

11 To work an edging, make a slip knot on the hook, insert the hook into the first loop along one edge, and work a single crochet stitch. Keeping the loops twisted in the same direction, work a single crochet into each loop along the edge, then fasten off the yarn. Repeat along the second edge.

EDGE FINISHES

AN EDGE FINISH IS A TYPE OF CROCHET EDGING THAT IS WORKED DIRECTLY ONTO THE EDGES OF ANOTHER PIECE OF CROCHET (AS OPPOSED TO BEING WORKED SEPARATELY AND THEN ATTACHED).

SEE ALSO
• Basic skills and stitches, pages 14–21
• Edgings, pages 108–109

The basic edge finish is a row of single crochet stitches, and this is often worked as a base before other, more decorative, edgings are worked. Crab stitch edging (also known as reversed single crochet) makes a hard-wearing knotted edge; shell edging adds a pretty, feminine finish to garments; and picot edging makes a delicately toothed edge.

WORKING A SINGLE CROCHET EDGING

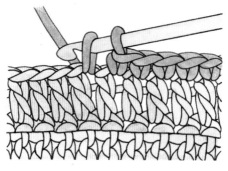

Working from right to left along the row, work a row of single crochet stitches into the edge of the crochet fabric, spacing the stitches evenly along the edge.

WORKING A CRAB STITCH EDGING

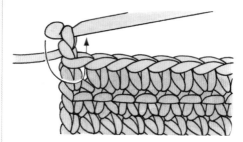

1 Unlike most other crochet techniques, this stitch is worked from left to right along the row. Keeping the yarn at the back of the work, insert the hook from front to back into the next stitch.

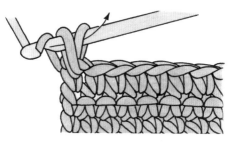

2 Wrap the yarn over the hook and draw the loop through to the front so that there are two loops on the hook. Wrap the yarn over the hook again, then draw the yarn through both loops to complete the stitch. Continue in this way along the edge.

Single crochet edging

Crab stitch edging

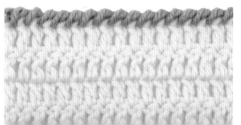

WORKING A SHELL EDGING

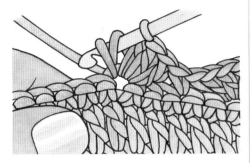

1 Work a foundation row of single crochet (a multiple of 6 stitches plus 1) into the edge of the crochet fabric, then make one chain and turn. Working from right to left along the row, work one single crochet into the first stitch, * skip the next two stitches, and then work five double crochet stitches into the next stitch to make a shell.

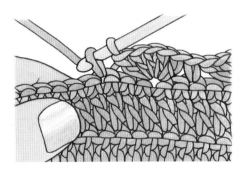

2 Skip two stitches and work a single crochet into the next stitch. Repeat from * along the edge.

WORKING A PICOT EDGING

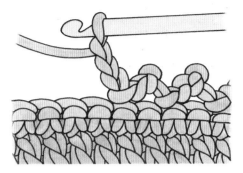

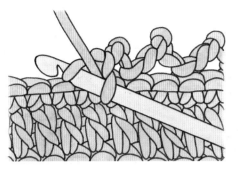

1 With wrong side facing, work a row of an even number of single crochet stitches along the edge and turn. * To work a picot, make three chains.

2 Insert the hook into the back of the third chain from the hook and work a slip stitch into it.

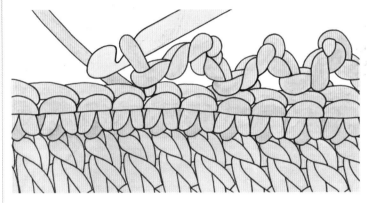

3 Working from right to left along the row, skip one stitch along the single crochet edge and work a slip stitch into the next single crochet. Repeat from * along the edge.

Shell edging

Picot edging

BUTTONHOLES AND BUTTON LOOPS

BANDS WITH BUTTONS, BUTTONHOLES, AND BUTTON LOOPS ARE BEST WORKED IN SINGLE CROCHET FOR STRENGTH AND NEATNESS. BUTTON LOOPS ARE A DECORATIVE ALTERNATIVE TO THE ORDINARY BUTTONHOLE, AND ARE ESPECIALLY SUITABLE FOR LACY GARMENTS.

SEE ALSO

- Basic skills and stitches, pages 14–21
- Edge finishes, pages 98–99

Make the button band first, mark the positions of the buttons with safety pins, and work the buttonhole (or button loop) band to match, making holes or loops opposite the safety pin markers.

WORKING BUTTONHOLES

To make a buttonhole band, work a row of evenly spaced single crochet stitches along the garment edge, with the right side of the garment facing you. Work additional rows of single crochet until the band is the required width for positioning the buttonholes (about half of the total width of the button band), ending with a wrong side row.

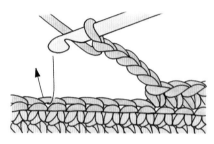

1 Work in single crochet to the position of the buttonhole, skip a few stitches to accommodate the size of the button, and work the same number of chains over the skipped stitches.

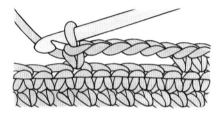

2 Anchor the chain by working a single crochet stitch after the skipped stitches. Continue in this way along the band until all the buttonholes have been worked.

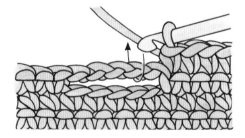

3 On the return (wrong side) row, work a single crochet into each stitch and work the same number of stitches into each chain loop as there are chains.

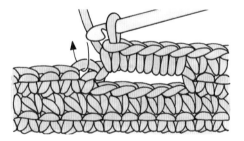

4 Continue along the row in this way, then work additional rows of single crochet until the buttonhole band is the same width as the button band.

WORKING BUTTON LOOPS

To make a band for button loops, work a row of evenly spaced single crochet stitches along the garment edge, with the right side of the garment facing you. Work additional rows of single crochet until the band is the required width, ending with a wrong side row. Bands for button loops are usually narrower than those with buttonholes.

Tip

Do not forget to space out all of the buttons at equal intervals on the button band first, then mark the positions of the corresponding buttonholes or loops on the opposite band to match.

CHOOSING BUTTONS

Buttons come in all shapes and sizes, and can add a unique touch to any crochet project. Take care to choose buttons that suit your project—for baby garments, choose small flat buttons; for adult garments or an accessory such as a purse, you can make a feature of one or more large decorative buttons. A button collection found in a thrift store can be a great bargain, and just one extraordinary button can even inspire a new project. To sew on buttons, use a sharp needle and matching yarn, or sewing thread in a matching or contrasting color.

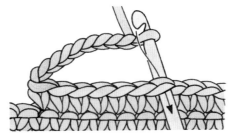

1 Work in single crochet to the position of the loop, then work several more stitches. Work a loop of chains to accommodate the button and turn it toward the right. Slip the hook out of the chain and insert it into the crochet at the point where you want the loop to finish.

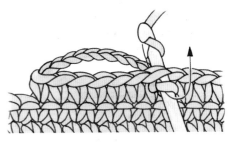

2 Insert the tip of the hook into the last chain, wrap the yarn over the hook, and join the loop to the band with a slip stitch.

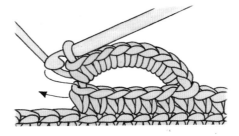

3 To complete the loop, work a series of single crochet stitches into the loop until the chain is completely covered.

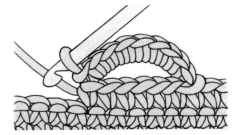

4 Insert the hook into the last single crochet worked before making the chain and work a slip stitch. Continue along the row in single crochet until all the loops have been worked.

CORDS

CROCHET CORDS CAN BE FLAT OR ROUNDED, NARROW OR WIDE. THEY ARE USED TO MAKE HANDLES AND SHOULDER STRAPS FOR PURSES, AND AS TIES TO SECURE A NECKLINE OR THE FRONT OF A GARMENT. NARROW CORD CAN BE SEWN ONTO A PLAIN PIECE OF CROCHET TO DECORATE IT WITH SHAPES SUCH AS SPIRALS, STRIPES, OR SWIRLS.

SEE ALSO

- Tubular crochet, pages 72–73

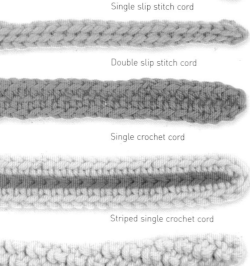

Single slip stitch cord

Double slip stitch cord

Single crochet cord

Striped single crochet cord

Round cord

When making a crochet cord, you will need to make the foundation chain longer than the finished cord you require, because the chain will contract as you work into it. Make several more inches of chain than you think you will need. Using slip stitch is the quickest and easiest way of making a narrow yet substantial cord that is good for making ties and using as decoration. The double slip stitch cord is wider than the single slip stitch version.

MAKING A SINGLE SLIP STITCH CORD

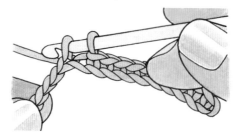

Work a foundation chain to the required length. Change to a size smaller hook, insert it into the second chain from the hook, and work a row of slip stitch along the top of the chain. You can alter the effect by working the slip stitch row into the back bumps of the chain rather than into one or both of the top loops.

MAKING A DOUBLE SLIP STITCH CORD

Work a foundation chain to the required length. Change to a size smaller hook, insert it into the second chain from the hook, and work a row of slip stitch along the first side of the chain. At the end of the first side, work one chain, turn, and continue along the second side of the chain in the same way.

MAKING A SINGLE CROCHET CORD

This makes a flat cord that is wider than a slip stitch cord. You can leave the cord plain or add a contrasting row of crochet down the center for added interest.

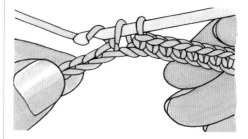

1 Work a foundation chain to the required length. Change to a size smaller hook, insert it into the second chain from the hook, and work a row of single crochet along one side of the chain.

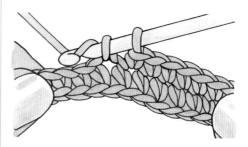

2 At the end of the first side, work one chain, turn, and continue along the second side of the chain in the same way.

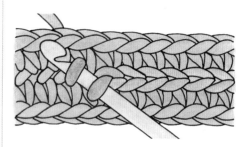

3 Using a contrast yarn, work a row of slip stitch down the center of the cord. You may need to use a larger hook size for the contrast yarn in order to prevent the stitches from puckering.

MAKING A ROUND CORD

Unlike the other types of crochet cord, this one is worked around and around in a continuous spiral of single crochet stitch until the cord is the required length. It makes a chunky cord that is good for purse handles and straps.

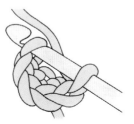

1 Make five chains and join into a ring with a slip stitch. Make one chain and then work a single crochet stitch into the top loop of the next chain.

2 Work one single crochet stitch into the top loop of each chain, then continue working around and around making one single crochet into the top loop of each stitch. As the cord grows, it will twist slightly into a spiral.

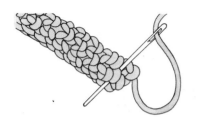

3 When the cord reaches the required length, fasten off the yarn. Thread the yarn end into a yarn or tapestry needle, catch the top loop of each stitch with the needle, and draw up the stitches to close the end of the spiral. Weave in the yarn end to finish. Close the beginning of the spiral in the same way.

CROCHET SPIRALS

Use a crochet spiral to trim a keyring or the tab on a zipper. You can make a large cluster of spirals to decorate each corner of a crochet throw as a novel alternative to a tassel. Experiment with different yarn combinations, such as a striped spiral in smooth yarn edged with a row of fluffy mohair or angora yarn.

MAKING A PLAIN SPIRAL

1 Work a loose foundation chain of 30 stitches. Change to a size smaller hook and work two double crochet stitches into the fourth chain from the hook. Continue along the chain, working four double crochet stitches into each chain.

2 As you work, the crochet will begin to twist naturally into a spiral formation. Fasten off the yarn at the end of the row, leaving a yarn end of about 12in (30cm) to attach the spiral.

MAKING A STRIPED SPIRAL

Using one color of yarn, work a plain spiral. Leave a long end for attaching the finished spiral. Join a contrasting yarn to the outer edge of the top of the spiral and work a row of single crochet stitches along the edge. Fasten off the ends of the contrast yarn.

Plain spiral

Striped spiral

FLOWERS

FLOWERS ARE QUICK TO MAKE, LOOK GREAT, AND CAN ADD THE FINISHING PERSONAL TOUCH TO ALL SORTS OF HOUSEHOLD ITEMS OR GARMENTS. DECORATE GARMENTS AND ACCESSORIES WITH SINGLE FLOWERS, OR WORK SEVERAL USING DIFFERENT COLORS AND YARNS AND ARRANGE THEM IN A GROUP.

SEE ALSO
- Basic skills and stitches, pages 14–21

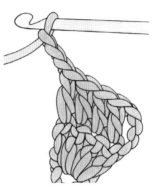

SMALL FLOWERS
These flowers have been worked in crochet cotton by adapting the cluster circle pattern (see page 79).

Tip
Sew-on embellishments such as flowers provide the perfect opportunity for experimenting with fancy and novelty yarns. Try combining textured and metallic yarns to make really unusual flowers.

MAKING A FRILLED FLOWER

1 Make the base of the first petal by working the required stitches into a foundation ring, then turn the work over so that the wrong side is facing you.

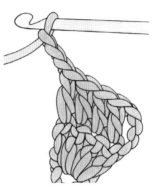

2 Work the remaining section of the petal into the base, then make three chains and turn the work so that the right side is facing you once more.

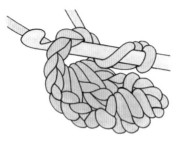

3 From the right side, take the hook and working yarn behind the petal just worked, and then work the first stitch of the new petal into the ring. This will fold the first petal into a three-dimensional shape. Continue working the rest of the round as instructed in the pattern.

MAKING A LAYERED FLOWER

1 Work the first round into a foundation ring, making eight central spokes to form the center of the flower. Work a round of petals into the chain spaces between the spokes. At the end of this round, break off the yarn.

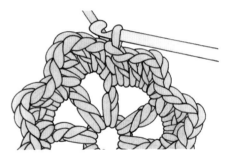

2 Make a slip knot on the hook with the second color and, working on the wrong side of the flower, insert the hook under one of the central spokes and slip stitch to join.

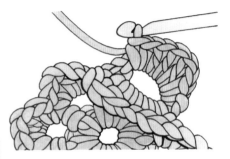

3 Work the final round of petals from the right side of the flower, folding over the petals you made on the second round to keep them out of the way of the hook.

Stitch collection

Frilled flower

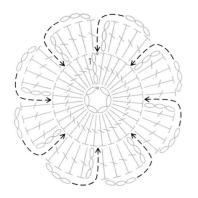

Pretty frilled petals make up this one-round flower. Each petal is completed and then folded over to make the frilled effect. Vary the flower by working it in a hand-painted yarn rather than a solid color.

FOUNDATION RING: Ch 6 and join with sl st to form a ring.

ROUND 1: Ch 3 (counts as 1 dc), 3 dc into ring, ch 3, turn; 1 dc into first dc, 1 dc into each of next 2 dc, 1 dc into 3rd of ch 3 (petal made), ch 3, turn; * working across back of petal just made, work 4 dc into ring, ch 3, turn; 1 dc into first dc, 1 dc into each of next 3 dc (petal made), ch 3, turn; rep from * 6 times, join with sl st into 3rd of beg ch 3 of first petal.
Fasten off yarn.

Layered flower

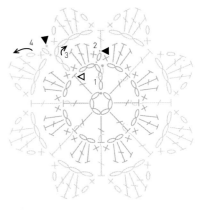

Layered flower

This flower looks pretty when two different types of yarn are used, so try combining a metallic yarn with a mohair yarn. The lower round of petals is worked behind the previous one to produce a three-dimensional effect.

YARN: Worked in two colors, A and B.

FOUNDATION RING: Using yarn A, ch 6 and join with sl st to form a ring.

ROUND 1: Ch 5 (counts as 1 dc, ch 2), [1 dc into ring, ch 2] 7 times, join with sl st into 3rd of ch 5.

ROUND 2: Sl st into next ch 2 sp, ch 1, [1 sc, 1 hdc, 1 dc, 1 hdc, 1 sc] into same sp (petal made), [1 sc, 1 hdc, 1 dc, 1 hdc, 1 sc] into each ch sp to end, join with sl st into first sc.
Break off yarn A. On the WS, join yarn B to one of the central spokes.

ROUND 3: Working on WS, ch 6 (counts as 1 dc, ch 3), [1 dc around next spoke, ch 3] 7 times, join with sl st into 3rd of ch 6.

ROUND 4: Ch 1, turn flower to RS, working behind petals of round 2, [1 sc, ch 1, 3 dc, ch 1, 1 sc] into each ch 3 sp to end [8 petals made], join with sl st into first sc.
Fasten off yarn.

Frilled flower

BRAIDS AND INSERTIONS

BRAIDS AND INSERTIONS ARE STRIPS OF CROCHET THAT CAN BE STITCHED TO OTHER PIECES OF CROCHET OR TO WOVEN FABRICS AS AN EMBELLISHMENT.

SEE ALSO
....
• Basic skills and stitches, pages 14–21

Making your own braids and insertions can be very rewarding. When using a small hook and fine cotton, cotton blend, or metallic yarn, the effect is similar to the purchased braids used to decorate home furnishings such as lampshades, pillows, and fabric-covered boxes and baskets. Using a matching sewing thread, hand stitch a braid to fabric using tiny stitches down the center or stitch an insertion along each edge. Provided the glue is compatible with the fiber composition of the yarn or thread, you can use a glue gun to attach braid to a box or basket.

BRAIDS

Braids are usually narrow, with both edges or at least one edge shaped rather than straight. Some braid patterns may be worked in more than one color of yarn.

INSERTIONS

Insertions are similar to braids but they tend to be narrow and have two straight edges. Often used for shaped lingerie (but not corsetry), these decorative lengths of crochet are often hand stitched between two pieces of fabric. Insertions have a practical as well as a decorative purpose. If worked in fine cotton or silk, the elasticity of the inserted crochet strip along a seam line adds some ease to the garment and makes the two pieces of fabric easier to join. Braid patterns can easily be adapted to become insertions by working lengths of chain between the shaped peaks of the braid edge and then perhaps working a row of single crochet stitches.

WORKING BRAIDS

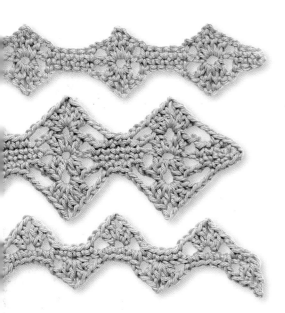

INSPIRATION FOR BRAID

These three braids are adaptations of the shell edging pattern (see page 109). To make the top braid, work the first row of the edging pattern along both sides of the foundation chain. For the middle braid, work both rows of the edging pattern along both sides of the foundation chain. To make the bottom braid, work one row of the edging pattern and offset the stitch repeat on the underside of the foundation chain.

1 Many braids are worked widthwise on a small number of stitches. Keep turning the braid and repeating the pattern row until it is the required length, then fasten off the yarn.

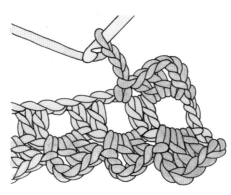

2 Fancy braid patterns worked in two or more colors usually have a foundation made in one color and a trim in a contrasting color. Work the first row of the contrasting trim along the top of the foundation, along the opposite side to the foundation chain.

3 Break off the contrast yarn and rejoin it on the other side of the foundation, then work this side to match the one already worked.

Stitch collection

Interwoven braid

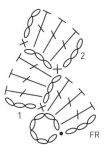

This braid is worked widthwise.

FOUNDATION RING: Ch 7 and join with sl st to form a ring.

FOUNDATION ROW: Ch 3, 3 dc into ring, ch 3, 1 sc into ring, turn.

ROW 1: Ch 3, 3 dc into ch 3 sp, ch 3, 1 sc into same ch 3 sp, turn.

Rep row 1 for length required.

Two-color braid

MULTIPLE OF 3 CHAINS

This braid is worked lengthwise.

YARN: Worked in two colors, A and B. Using yarn A, make the required length of foundation chain.

FOUNDATION ROW: 1 dc into 6th ch from hook, 1 dc into next ch, * ch 1, sk next ch, 1 dc into each of next 2 chs; rep from * to last 2 chs, ch 1, sk next ch, 1 dc into last ch. Break off yarn A and join yarn B to penultimate ch of beg skipped ch.

ROW 1: Ch 1, 1 sc into first ch sp, ch 3, 2 dc into same ch sp, * [1 sc, ch 3, 2 dc] into next ch 1 sp; rep from * to last dc, 1 sc into last dc.

Break off yarn B and rejoin yarn B to opposite side of braid with sl st into foundation ch below first dc.

ROW 2: Ch 1, 1 sc into first ch sp, ch 3, 2 dc into same ch sp, * [1 sc, ch 3, 2 dc] into next ch 1 sp; rep from * ending last rep with 1 sc into 2nd ch of last ch sp. Fasten off yarn.

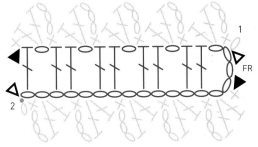

EDGINGS

EDGINGS ARE USED TO TRIM THE
EDGES OF OTHER PIECES OF CROCHET
OR WOVEN FABRICS. UNLIKE EDGE
FINISHES THAT ARE WORKED DIRECTLY
ONTO THE CROCHET FABRIC, THE
EDGINGS DESCRIBED HERE ARE WORKED
SEPARATELY AND THEN ATTACHED.

SEE ALSO
• Basic skills and
  stitches, pages 14–21
• Edge finishes,
  pages 98–99

Edgings usually have one straight and one
shaped edge. Deep edgings are also known as
borders. Edgings can be worked in short rows
across the width of the crochet piece or in long
rows across the length. When working edgings
in long rows, it is a good idea to make a longer
chain than you think you will need and unravel
the unused chains after the edging is finished.

CORNERS

There is a simple trick to remember for
working edgings around corners. Count a
corner stitch as either three or five stitches
and work the required next three or five
stitches of the repeat into the corner stitch.
The number of stitches that should be worked
into the corner stitch can vary, so it is always
advisable to try out an edging on a swatch of
the fabric to which it will eventually be applied.

To plan what part of the edging repeat will be
worked into the corner stitches, work a swatch
of the edging in the yarn to be used, lay it along
the edge to be embellished, and use pins to
mark out the repeats around the corner as well
as the start and finish positions of the first and
last repeats.

ADAPTING EDGE FINISHES

This chain loop edge finish has
been worked directly onto the
project, but it could have been
worked along a foundation row
of single crochet stitches as
a separate edging and then
stitched to the crochet fabric.

USING AN APPROXIMATE FOUNDATION CHAIN

When working long edgings that are to be hand
stitched to a fabric, it is often useful to make an
approximate foundation chain, then work a row
of the pattern and stretch or ease the edging to
the nearest repeat.

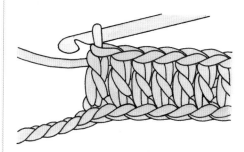

1 Make the foundation chain and work the
appropriate number of repeats of your edging
pattern. At this point, turn and continue the
pattern, leaving any surplus chains unworked.

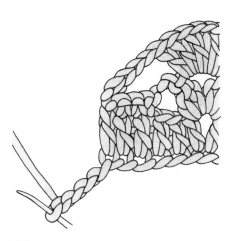

2 When the border is complete, snip off the slip
knot at the end of the unworked chains. Using a
yarn or tapestry needle, carefully unravel the
chains until you reach the edge of the work, then
weave in the yarn end on the wrong side.

Stitch collection

Shell edging

> MULTIPLE OF 10 CHAINS PLUS 3

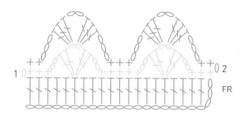

This edging is worked lengthwise.

FOUNDATION ROW: (RS) 1 dc into 4th ch from hook, 1 dc into each ch to end.

ROW 1: Ch 1, 1 sc into each of first 3 dc, * ch 2, sk next 2 dc, [2 dc, ch 2] twice into next dc, sk next 2 dc, 1 sc into each of next 5 dc; rep from * to end omitting 2 sc at end of last rep and working last sc into top of beg skipped ch 3, turn.

ROW 2: Ch 1, 1 sc into each of first 2 sc, * ch 3, sk next ch 2 sp, [3 dc, ch 2, 3 dc] into next ch 2 sp, ch 3, sk next sc, 1 sc into each of next 3 sc; rep from * to end omitting 1 sc at end of last rep.
Fasten off yarn.

Deep mesh edging

This edging is worked widthwise.

FOUNDATION CHAIN: Ch 20.

FOUNDATION ROW: (RS) 1 dc into 4th ch from hook, 1 dc into each of next 2 chs, * ch 1, sk next ch, 1 dc into next ch; rep from * to end, turn.

ROW 1: Ch 7, 1 dc into first dc, [ch 1, 1 dc into next dc] 7 times, 1 dc into each of next 2 dc, 1 dc into 3rd of beg skipped ch 3, turn.

ROW 2: Ch 3 (counts as 1 dc), 1 dc into each of next 3 dc, * ch 1, 1 dc into next dc; rep from * to end, turn.

ROW 3: Ch 7, 1 dc into first dc, [ch 1, 1 dc into next dc] 7 times, 1 dc into each of next 2 dc, 1 dc into 3rd of ch 3, turn.

Rep rows 2 and 3 for desired length, ending with a row 3.

KEY TO ABBREVIATIONS AND SYMBOLS pages 150–151

FRINGES AND TASSELS

AS A CHANGE FROM THE USUAL YARN FRINGE OF THE TYPE FOUND ON SCARVES, TRY MAKING ONE OF THESE CROCHET FRINGES OR TASSELS. NEARLY EVERY FRINGE PATTERN CAN BE ADAPTED TO MAKE TO A TASSEL.

SEE ALSO
• Basic skills and stitches, pages 14–21
• Edgings, pages 108–109

A chain fringe or tassel is made from loops of crochet chain, while a corkscrew fringe or tassel is made from strips of single crochet worked so that they curl around and around.

WORKING A CROCHET CHAIN FRINGE

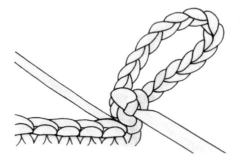

On the fringe row, make 15 chains and join the end of the chain with a slip stitch into the same place as the previous crochet stitch.

WORKING A CORKSCREW FRINGE

To make the corkscrew shapes, make 15 chains and turn. Work two single crochet stitches into the second chain from the hook and into each remaining chain.

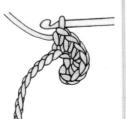

CORKSCREW TASSEL

To make this corkscrew tassel, work rows 1 and 2 of the chain loop tassel opposite, and then work row 2 to the required depth. Finish by working the fringe row, but replace the chain loop with a chain approximately twice the required length and work three double crochet stitches into each chain.

Chain fringe

> ANY NUMBER OF CHAINS

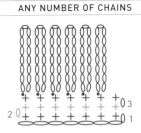

This fringe is worked lengthwise.

FOUNDATION CHAIN: Make the required length of foundation chain.

ROW 1: 1 sc into 2nd ch from hook, 1 sc into each ch to end, turn.

ROW 2: Ch 1, 1 sc into each sc to end, turn.

ROW 3: Ch 1, 1 sc into first sc, * 1 sc into next sc, ch 15, sl st into same place as sc just worked; rep from * to end.

Fasten off yarn.

Corkscrew fringe

ANY NUMBER OF CHAINS

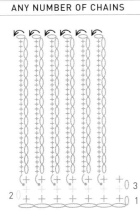

This fringe is worked lengthwise.

FOUNDATION CHAIN: Make the required length of foundation chain.

ROW 1: 1 sc into 2nd ch from hook, 1 sc into each ch to end, turn.

ROW 2: Ch 1, 1 sc into each sc to end, turn.

ROW 3: Ch 1, 1 sc into first sc, * 1 sc into next sc, ch 15, turn; working back along the chain, sk first ch, 2 sc into each rem ch, sl st into same place as sc before the ch 15; rep from * to end.

Fasten off yarn.

Chain loop tassel

FOUNDATION CHAIN: Leaving a long tail, ch 19.

ROW 1: 1 sc into 2nd ch from hook, 1 sc into each ch to end, turn.

ROW 2: Ch 1, sk first sc, 1 sc into each sc to end, 1 sc into ch 1, turn.

ROW 3: Ch 2, sk first sc, * hdc4tog into next sc, ch 1, 1 hdc into next sc; rep from * ending with 1 hdc into ch 1, turn.

ROW 4: Ch 1, sk [first hdc and ch 1] * 1 sc into hdc4tog, sk next hdc, 1 sc into ch sp; rep from * ending with 1 sc into top of ch 2, turn.

FRINGE ROW: Ch 1, [1 sc, ch 36, 1 sl st] into each sc ending with [1 sc, ch 36, 1 sl st] into ch 1.

Fasten off yarn, leaving a long tail.

Tightly roll up the rows of sc and use the starting tail to stitch firmly across the top of the tassel head through all the layers, ending with a stitch in the center. Use the finishing tail to stitch in and out around the base of the roll and draw tight. Secure with a back stitch, then join the side edge of the roll and bring the tail out at the center top. Use the two tails to secure the tassel where required.

SURFACE CROCHET

SURFACE CROCHET IS EXACTLY AS THE NAME SUGGESTS: CROCHET WORKED ON TOP OF A CROCHET BACKGROUND. YOU CAN WORK ON PLAIN SINGLE CROCHET FABRIC, BUT THE LINES OF SURFACE SLIP STITCH LOOK MUCH MORE EFFECTIVE WORKED ON A MESH BACKGROUND.

SEE ALSO

• Openwork and lace stitches, pages 52–55

ADDING COLOR
Try mixing metallic and smooth yarns.

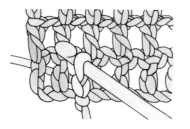

Choose a smooth yarn to make the mesh background, then add rows of contrasting colors and textures to the surface using this simple, but effective, technique.

WORKING SURFACE CROCHET

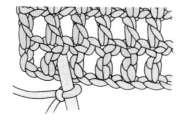

1 Work a mesh background. Make a slip knot in the contrasting yarn and slip it onto the hook. Insert the hook through a hole along the lower edge of the mesh.

2 Holding the contrast yarn behind the mesh, draw a loop of yarn through the mesh and through the loop on the hook to make a slip stitch. Continue in this way, working up the mesh and making one slip stitch in each hole.

3 At the top of the row, break off the yarn and pull it through the last stitch to secure.

Stitch collection

Openwork mesh

> MULTIPLE OF 2 CHAINS PLUS 4

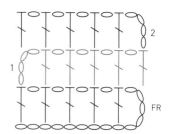

To make the mesh background, work a piece of fabric in the openwork mesh pattern (see page 53). Work vertical rows of surface crochet to make solid stripes across the background. This mesh has fairly large holes, so it is a good idea to use a heavier weight of yarn to work the surface crochet than the one used for the background.

Tip

As well as the two mesh background stitches shown here, you can use other crochet stitches as a background for this technique, including single and half double crochet, but remember not to work the background stitches too tightly.

Small mesh

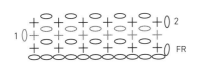

MULTIPLE OF 2 CHAINS

This background fabric has much smaller holes than the larger openwork mesh example. You can work surface crochet in rows on this fabric, but the smaller mesh means that you can experiment and work all sorts of random patterns like those shown here.

FOUNDATION ROW: (RS) 1 sc into 2nd ch from hook, * ch 1, sk next ch, 1 sc into next ch; rep from * to end, turn.

ROW 1: Ch 1, 1 sc into first sc, * ch 1, 1 sc into next sc; rep from * to end, turn. Rep row 1 for length required.

Small mesh

ADDING TEXTURE
Try working surface crochet with a contrasting yarn texture in a freestyle design.

Openwork mesh

KEY TO ABBREVIATIONS AND SYMBOLS pages 150–151

APPLYING BEADS

BEADS CAN BE APPLIED TO CROCHET AT THE SAME TIME AS THE STITCHES ARE BEING WORKED. THEY LOOK MOST EFFECTIVE AGAINST A SINGLE CROCHET BACKGROUND, AND ADD TOUCHES OF COLOR AS WELL AS GLITZ AND SPARKLE.

SEE ALSO

• Applying sequins, pages 116–117

BEADS
Choose beads to match your yarn.

Before starting to crochet, thread all of the beads onto the ball of yarn. If you are using several balls, the pattern will tell you how many beads to thread onto each ball. When working with several bead colors in a particular sequence, you need to thread them onto the yarn in reverse order, so that the pattern will be correct as you crochet.

BEADING WITH SINGLE CROCHET

1 Work to the position of the first bead on a wrong side row. Slide the bead down the yarn until it rests snugly against the right side of the work.

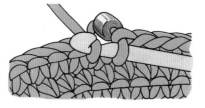

2 Keeping the bead in position, insert the hook into the next stitch and draw the yarn through so that there are two loops on the hook.

3 Wrap the yarn over the hook again and draw it through to complete the stitch. Continue adding beads in this way across the row, following pattern instructions.

Stitch collection

All-over beads

MULTIPLE OF 4 CHAINS PLUS 4

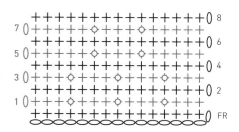

Beads added to every wrong side row make a heavily beaded fabric that would be perfect for making an evening purse. You could also work several rows of this pattern in a narrow band around the hem of a sweater. This stitch pattern uses several colors of beads threaded randomly onto the yarn. Thread all of the beads onto the yarn before starting to crochet.

NOTE: B = beaded single crochet stitch.
FOUNDATION ROW: (RS) 1 sc into 2nd ch from hook, 1 sc into each ch to end, turn.
ROW 1: (WS BEAD ROW) Ch 1, 1 sc into each of first 3 sc, * B, 1 sc into each of next 3 sc; rep from * to last 4 sc, B, 1 sc into each of next 3 sc, turn.
ROW 2: Ch 1, 1 sc into each sc to end, turn.
ROWS 3–4: Rep rows 1 and 2.
ROW 5: (WS BEAD ROW) Ch 1, 1 sc into each of next 5 sc, * B, 1 sc into each of next 3 sc; rep from * to last 6 sc, B, 1 sc into each of next 5 sc, turn.
ROW 6: Ch 1, 1 sc into each sc to end, turn.
ROWS 7–8: Rep rows 5 and 6.
Rep rows 1–8 for length required, ending with a RS row.

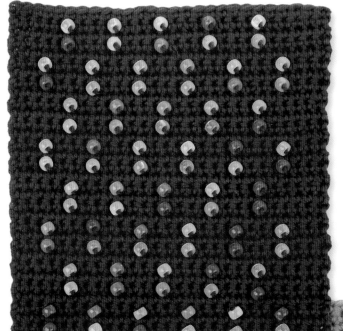

All-over beads

Alternate beads

MULTIPLE OF 6 CHAINS PLUS 4

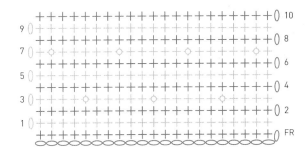

Beads of one color are arranged alternately to make this elegant beaded pattern. Use matte beads, like those shown, or choose from metallic and glitter types to add more sparkle. Thread all of the beads onto the yarn before starting to crochet.

NOTE: B = beaded single crochet stitch.

FOUNDATION ROW: (RS) 1 sc into 2nd ch from hook, 1 sc into each ch to end, turn.

ROWS 1–2: Ch 1, 1 sc into each sc to end, turn.

ROW 3: (WS BEAD ROW) Ch 1, 1 sc into each of next 4 sc, * B, 1 sc into each of next 5 sc; rep from * to last 5 sc, B, 1 sc into each of next 4 sc, turn.

ROWS 4–6: Rep row 1.

ROW 7: (WS BEAD ROW) Ch 1, 1 sc into first sc, * B, 1 sc into each of next 5 sc; rep from * to last 2 sc, B, 1 sc into last sc, turn.

ROWS 8–10: Rep row 1.

Rep rows 3–10 for length required, ending with a row 5.

Tip
When choosing beads, match the size of the holes in the beads to the thickness of the yarn. Small beads are best on fine yarns, and larger beads on bulky yarns.

Alternate beads

KEY TO ABBREVIATIONS AND SYMBOLS pages 150–151

APPLYING SEQUINS

SEQUINS CAN BE APPLIED TO A BACKGROUND OF SINGLE CROCHET IN A SIMILAR WAY TO BEADS. ROUND SEQUINS, EITHER FLAT OR CUP-SHAPED, ARE THE BEST ONES TO USE.

When crocheting with cup-shaped sequins, make sure that you thread them onto the yarn so that the convex side (the bottom of the "cup") of each sequin faces the same way toward the ball of yarn. When crocheted, the "cup" should face away from the crochet fabric. This displays the sequin to best advantage and also prevents it from damaging the crochet. As a general rule, thread sequins onto the yarn in the same way as beads.

SEE ALSO

• Applying beads, pages 114–115

ALTERNATE SEQUINS
This crochet sample is made using the alternate beads pattern (see page 119) but with sequins instead of beads.

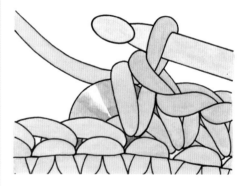

ADDING SEQUINS TO SINGLE CROCHET

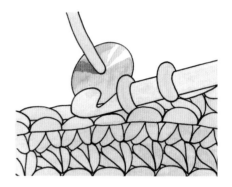

1 Work to the position of the first sequin on a wrong side row. Work the first stage of the single crochet, leaving two loops on the hook. Slide the sequin down the yarn until it rests snugly against the right side of the work. If you are using cup-shaped sequins, remember that the convex side (the bottom of the "cup") should be next to the fabric.

2 Keeping the sequin in position, wrap the yarn over the hook and draw it through to complete the stitch. Continue adding sequins in this way across the row, following the pattern instructions.

Stitch collection

Sequin stripes

MULTIPLE OF 6 CHAINS PLUS 3

Sequins often look best when used sparingly to accentuate a design. Here, flat round sequins in one color are arranged in neat vertical rows so that the sequins touch. You can use a contrasting sequin color or match them to the background fabric for a more subtle effect. Thread all of the sequins onto the yarn before starting to crochet.

NOTE: S = sequined single crochet stitch.

FOUNDATION ROW: (RS) 1 sc into 2nd ch from hook, 1 sc into each ch to end, turn.

ROWS 1–2: Ch 1, 1 sc into each sc to end, turn.

ROW 3: (WS SEQUIN ROW) Ch 1, 1 sc into each of next 3 sc, * S, 1 sc into each of next 5 sc; rep from * to last 5 sc, S, 1 sc into each of next 4 sc, turn.

ROW 4: Ch 1, 1 sc into each sc to end, turn. Rep rows 3 and 4 for length required, ending with a row 4.

Tip

Knitting sequins have larger holes than ordinary ones, and they are often sold threaded onto a loop of strong thread. To use the sequins, cut the loop, knot one end of the thread onto the yarn, and carefully slide the sequins over the knot and onto the yarn.

KEY TO ABBREVIATIONS AND SYMBOLS **pages 150–151**

CHAPTER THREE
· ·
Projects

This chapter shows you how to make a variety of projects using the skills you have mastered in the previous two chapters. Whether you want to make a small crochet accessory such as a pretty scarf or flower-trimmed bag, or feel ready to try something a little more complicated, there is something here for everyone.

BUTTONHOLE BAG

BRIGHTLY COLORED FLOWERS AND LEAVES TRIM A PLAIN BUTTONHOLE BAG THAT IS LARGE ENOUGH TO HOLD WALLET, KEYS, CELL PHONE, AND OTHER ESSENTIALS. THE BAG PATTERN ALSO LOOKS GOOD WITHOUT THE ADDED TRIMMINGS, AND IT CAN BE WORKED IN ONE COLOR OR IN STRIPES.

YOU WILL NEED

- 4 balls of double knitting yarn with approx. 131yds (120m) per 50g ball in a neutral color
- Oddments of same yarn in red, yellow, and green
- Size F (4mm), J (6mm), and K (6.5mm) crochet hooks, or sizes needed to achieve gauge
- Yarn or tapestry needle

EMBELLISHMENT

Decorating with sew-on motifs allows you to add as little or as much embellishment to the bag as you like.

GAUGE

14 stitches and 17 rows to 4in (10cm) measured over single crochet worked using size J (6mm) crochet hook and two strands of main yarn held together.

FINISHED SIZE

10in (25cm) high and 10½in (27cm) wide.

FRONT PANEL

Using size K (6.5mm) hook and holding two strands of main yarn together, ch 37. Change to size J (6mm) hook.

FOUNDATION ROW: (RS) 1 sc into 2nd ch from hook, 1 sc into each ch to end, turn.

ROW 1: Ch 1, 1 sc into each sc to end, turn. (36 sc)

Rep last row 30 times more, ending with a RS row.

MAKING THE BUTTONHOLE

ROW 1: (WS) Ch 1, 1 sc into each of next 12 sc, ch 12, sk next 12 sc, 1 sc into each of next 12 sc, turn.

ROW 2: Ch 1, 1 sc into each of next 12 sc, 1 sc into each of next 12 chs, sk next 12 sc, 1 sc into each of next 12 sc, turn. (36 sc)

MAKING THE HANDLE

ROW 1: (WS) Ch 1, 1 sc into each sc to end, turn. Rep last row three times more, ending with a RS row.
Fasten off yarn.

BACK PANEL

Work as for front panel.

FLOWERS AND LEAVES

Using size F (4mm) hook and a single strand of contrast yarn, make three red and three yellow frilled flowers (see page 105).
Using size F (4mm) hook and green yarn, make two short lengths of single crochet cord (see page 102).

FINISHING

Weave in the yarn ends (see page 25), then press the pieces lightly on the wrong side (see pages 28–29). Pin flowers and leaves to front panel, making sure that flowers overlap ends of leaves. Secure flowers with a few stitches worked in matching yarn, taking the stitches over the chains behind each flower petal. Stitch leaves in place down the center of each leaf. Place front and back panels right sides together and pin around the edges. Using matching yarn, join side and base seams (see pages 30–31), then turn bag right side out.

INTARSIA POTHOLDER

COMBINE ODDMENTS OF DOUBLE KNITTING YARN WITH ONE BALL OF MAIN COLOR TO MAKE THIS CHEERFUL INTARSIA POTHOLDER. THE BACK PIECE IS WORKED IN SINGLE CROCHET USING THE MAIN COLOR, BUT YOU COULD WORK TWO PATTERNED PIECES IF YOU PREFER.

YOU WILL NEED
- 1 ball of double knitting yarn with approx. 131yds (120m) per 50g ball in main color (A)
- Oddments of same yarn in four toning colors (B, C, D, and E)
- Size F (4mm) and G (4.5mm) crochet hooks, or sizes needed to achieve gauge
- Yarn or tapestry needle

GAUGE
17 stitches and 21 rows to 4in (10cm) measured over single crochet worked using size F (4mm) crochet hook.

FINISHED SIZE
Approximately 7in (19cm) square, including edge finish but excluding hanging loop.

FRONT PANEL
Using size G (4.5mm) hook and yarn A, ch 31. Change to size F (4mm) hook. Following guidelines for working intarsia (see pages 70–71), work the pattern from the chart (see right), reading upward from the bottom. Start at the right-hand edge and read right side (odd-numbered) rows from right to left and wrong side (even-numbered) rows from left to right. When the chart has been completed, fasten off yarn.

BACK PANEL
Using size G (4.5mm) hook and yarn A, ch 31. Change to size F (4mm) hook.
FOUNDATION ROW: (RS) 1 sc into 2nd ch from hook, 1 sc into each ch to end, turn. (30 sc)
ROW 1: Ch 1, 1 sc into each sc to end, turn. Rep last row 32 times more, ending with a WS row.
Fasten off yarn.

FINISHING
Weave in the yarn ends (see page 25), then block each panel to same size (see pages 28–29). Place panels wrong sides together and pin around the edges. With front piece facing, join yarn A to one corner of potholder.
ROUND 1: (RS) Ch 1, 1 sc into same place, work evenly spaced sc all around edge of potholder working 3 sc into each corner, join with sl st into first sc.

STASH BUSTER
This is the ideal project for using up some of the oddments of yarn that you have in your stash.

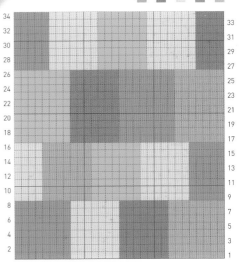

A B C D E

ROUND 2: Make hanging loop (ch 9, insert hook into last st of previous round and work sl st), ch 1, 15 sc into loop, 1 sc into each sc around edge of potholder working 3 sc into center stitch of 3 sc group at each corner, join with sl st into first sc of loop.
Fasten off yarn and weave in yarn ends.

BABY AFGHAN

AN AFGHAN FOR A NEW BABY IS ALWAYS A POPULAR GIFT. THIS DESIGN IS FAIRLY SMALL, BUT YOU CAN EASILY MAKE IT LARGER SIMPLY BY ADDING MORE MOTIFS BEFORE YOU WORK THE EDGE FINISH. IF YOU DO THIS, REMEMBER THAT YOU WILL NEED TO BUY MORE YARN THAN THE AMOUNT SUGGESTED HERE.

YOU WILL NEED
- 5 balls of double knitting yarn with approx. 131yds (120m) per 50g ball in 3 coordinating colors: 1 ball of pale green, 2 balls of white, 2 balls of pale yellow
- Size E (3.5mm) and F (4mm) crochet hooks, or sizes needed to achieve gauge
- Yarn or tapestry needle

GAUGE
After blocking, each motif measures 5in (14cm) square.

FINISHED SIZE
18in (48cm) wide and 28in (72cm) long, including edge finish.

MOTIFS
Using size F (4mm) hook, follow the pattern for the Croydon square (see page 82).

MOTIF A (MAKE 8)
Use white as yarn A, pale green as yarn B, and pale yellow as yarn C.

MOTIF B (MAKE 7)
Use pale yellow as yarn A, pale green as yarn B, and white as yarn C.

MAKING UP THE AFGHAN
Weave in the yarn ends (see page 25), then block each motif to same size (see pages 28–29). Arrange motifs as shown in diagram below and stitch together using matching yarn (see pages 80–81).

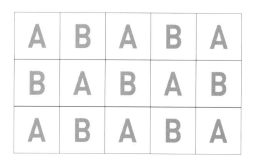

A	B	A	B	A
B	A	B	A	B
A	B	A	B	A

ADJUSTING THE SIZE
The baby afghan is worked as separate square motifs that are stitched together, so it can easily be made larger.

EDGE FINISH

Using size E (3.5mm) hook, join pale yellow yarn to any sc along edge of afghan.

ROUND 1: Ch 3, 1 dc into each sc around afghan working 5 dc into center stitch of 3 sc group at each corner, join with sl st into 3rd of ch 3. Break off pale yellow yarn and join white yarn in same place.

ROUND 2: Ch 3, 1 dc into each dc working 5 dc into center stitch of 5 dc group at each corner, join with sl st into 3rd of ch 3. Break off white yarn and join pale green yarn in same place.

ROUND 3: Ch 1, 1 sc into same place, 1 sc into each dc working 3 sc into center stitch of 5 dc group at each corner, join with sl st into first sc.

Fasten off yarn.

FINISHING

Press edge finish lightly on wrong side with warm iron or block the afghan again.

BLANKET SIZE

It is a good idea to make a baby blanket that is just big enough for a cot or stroller.

USING A DIFFERENT MOTIF

For a baby afghan, there are a few practical issues to consider. First, choose a yarn that is both washable and does not have long, loose fibers. In addition, select a yarn that will break if it is pulled sharply. This does not mean that the afghan will not be hard wearing, but if a small child decides to twist the blanket with his or her fingers, those fingers are less likely to become trapped. Another measure to safeguard against trapped fingers is to choose a design with large holes rather than one with long chains that are not worked over or into on subsequent rounds.

A multicolored blanket can be more forgiving between washes. A colorful blanket will also appeal more to the baby, and it provides an excellent opportunity for using up oddments of yarn.

ALTERNATIVE MOTIF

You can choose a different square motif to make the afghan if you prefer. This circle in a square motif (see page 83) would look good worked in a single color or in several colors.

HEXAGON PILLOW

MAKING A PILLOW COVER FROM MOTIFS IS A GREAT WAY TO SHOW OFF YOUR CROCHET SKILLS. IN THIS PATTERN, 24 HEXAGONS WORKED IN A NEUTRAL PALETTE ARE JOINED TOGETHER TO MAKE A RECTANGULAR COVER. YOU CAN USE A COORDINATING COLOR SCHEME LIKE THAT FEATURED HERE, OR WORK EACH HEXAGON IN A DIFFERENT COLOR USING ODDMENTS OF YARN FROM YOUR STASH.

HEXAGON MOTIFS
You could replace the wheel hexagon motif used here with the classic or granny hexagon (see pages 87 and 89), but work each one in a single color rather than in three colors.

YOU WILL NEED
- Shetland double knitting yarn with approx. 134yds (122m) per 50g ball in 7 coordinating colors: 1 ball each of mustard (A), rust (B), cream (C), and lemon (G); 2 balls each of gold (D), brown (E), and nutmeg (F)
- Size F (4mm) crochet hook, or size needed to achieve gauge
- Yarn or tapestry needle
- 16 x 20in (40 x 50cm) pillow form

GAUGE
After blocking, each motif measures 5in (13cm) from side to side and 5¾in (14.5cm) from point to point.

FINISHED SIZE
Fits a 16 x 20in (40 x 50cm) pillow form.

MOTIFS
Using the wheel hexagon pattern (see page 88), work three motifs in each of yarns A, B, C, and G, and four motifs in each of yarns D, E, and F.

FINISHING
Weave in the yarn ends (see page 25), then block each motif to same size (see pages 28–29). Arrange motifs as shown in diagram below, then stitch together using matching yarn (see pages 30–31). When the motifs have been joined, fold the crochet to the back following the dotted lines on the diagram and join the edges of the remaining motifs. Leave the motif edges numbered 1, 2, 3, and 4 on the diagram unstitched to make the opening on the back of the cover. Turn cover right side out and insert pillow form. Matching the edges of the motifs along the opening, pin and stitch carefully together.

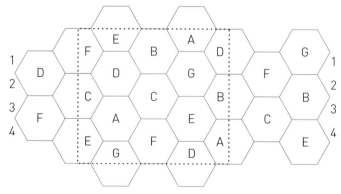

·········· Fold line

COLOR INSPIRATION
The color palette for
this pillow was inspired
by the fall landscape.

WARM COLORS
The color of this scarf will reflect flattering warm pink onto the skin.

WINTER SCARF

A SCARF MAKES THE PERFECT PROJECT FOR A BEGINNER TO CROCHET. THERE IS NO SHAPING, THE WORK IS NARROW ENOUGH TO GROW QUICKLY, AND YOU CAN CHOOSE FROM MANY OF THE PATTERNS FEATURED IN THE STITCH COLLECTIONS THROUGHOUT THIS BOOK. THE SCARF SHOWN HERE IS WORKED IN A FAN LACE PATTERN USING A PURE WOOL YARN.

YOU WILL NEED
• 2 balls of double knitting yarn with approx. 131yds (120m) per 50g ball
• Size F (4mm) and G (4.5mm) crochet hooks, or sizes needed to achieve gauge
• Yarn or tapestry needle

GAUGE
After blocking, one complete pattern repeat measures 2in (6cm) wide and 1in (3cm) deep.

FINISHED SIZE
After blocking, approximately 7in (18cm) wide and 46in (117cm) long.

FAN LACE PATTERN
The stitch pattern for fan lace (see page 55) requires a multiple of 12 chains plus 3. The scarf shown here was worked on a foundation chain of 39 = (12 x 3) + 3.
Using size G (4.5mm) hook, ch 39.
Change to size F (4mm) hook and work in pattern for approximately 46in (117cm), ending with a row 4.

FINISHING
Weave in the yarn ends (see page 25), then block the scarf (see pages 28–29).

**OPENWORK MESH
(SEE PAGE 53)**
This stitch is very easy to
work and has good drape.
It requires a multiple of 2 chains
plus 4 and this swatch was worked
on a foundation of 36 chains.

USING A DIFFERENT STITCH

Stitch patterns need a specific number of stitches
for the pattern to work correctly. When using a
different stitch to make the scarf, simply make
the foundation chain to the required number and
work a strip to the length you require.

**SEASHORE TRELLIS
(SEE PAGE 55)**
This very pretty pattern looks
good worked in ombré yarn. It
requires a multiple of 12 chains
plus 4 and this swatch was worked
on a foundation of 40 chains. This
is one more chain than the scarf in
the photograph, but the swatch is
narrower than the scarf due to the
difference in stitch construction.

**WAVY CHEVRONS
(SEE PAGE 63)**
Any of the chevron stitches on pages
61–63 would make an attractive scarf,
whether worked in one color or striped
in several toning or contrasting yarns.
Wavy chevron stitch requires a multiple
of 14 chains plus 3 and this swatch was
worked on a foundation of 45 chains.

TRINITY STITCH (SEE PAGE 41)
This cluster pattern makes a denser,
heavier fabric than the mesh or trellis
patterns, and would make a warmer
scarf than any of the lace stitches.
It requires a multiple of 2 chains
and this swatch was worked
on a foundation of
34 chains.

FILET CROCHET WRAP

FILET CROCHET CREATES A DELIGHTFUL LACY ACCESSORY. WORKED IN ROWS ACROSS THE WIDTH OF THE WRAP, EACH END IS DECORATED WITH A PRETTY BORDER PATTERN. THE MAIN PART OF THE WRAP IS IN FILET MESH, DOTTED HERE AND THERE WITH TINY FOUR-BLOCK MOTIFS.

YOU WILL NEED

- 8 balls of double knitting yarn with approx. 131yds (120m) per 50g ball
- Size F (4mm) and G (4.5mm) crochet hooks, or sizes needed to achieve gauge
- Yarn or tapestry needle

GAUGE

Approx. eight spaces to 4in (10cm) measured widthwise and lengthwise over filet mesh worked using size F (4mm) hook.

FINISHED SIZE

Approximately 23in (58cm) wide and 67in (170cm) long.

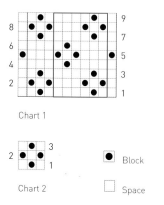

Chart 1

Chart 2

● Block

□ Space

FILET PATTERN

Using size G (4.5mm) hook, ch 146. Change to size F (4mm) hook and, following the guidelines for working filet crochet on pages 56–58, work two rows of spaces. Begin working the border pattern from chart 1 (above), repeating the section of the chart inside the red lines six times more. Work upward from the bottom of the chart, starting at the right-hand edge and reading right side (odd-numbered) rows from right to left and wrong side (even-numbered) rows from left to right. At the end of the border pattern, work in filet mesh, dotting several repeats of the tiny motif from chart 2 (left) at random across the mesh. Continue until work measures approximately 62in (157cm) long, ending with a WS row. Work the border chart once more, then finish by working two rows of spaces to match the opposite end.

FINISHING

Weave in the yarn ends (see page 25), then block the wrap or press lightly on the wrong side (see pages 28–29).

USING A DIFFERENT FILET CROCHET DESIGN

Designing the perfect wrap can mean making it the perfect size, using your favorite color, treating yourself to a special hank of yarn, or using images in your design that have a special meaning to you. The filet crochet technique can be used to work any design charted on a square grid in a single color. Many multicolored designs can be converted to a single color. As well as traditional filet crochet table mat and curtain motifs, cross-stitch designs and knitting patterns are also good sources of inspiration. Filet crochet looks good worked in almost any fiber, and can be quickly embellished with beads, surface crochet, or with fiber strands woven through the mesh. Quick to work, filet crochet is a very versatile crochet technique.

FILET CROCHET WORKED IN BULKY YARN

The use of a bulky yarn gives a modern twist to traditional filet crochet designs.

EVENING WEAR
Filet crochet creates a
lacy fabric, perfect for
evening wear.

STRIPED BAG

USE ODDMENTS OF YARN FROM YOUR STASH TO MAKE THIS PRETTY DRAWSTRING BAG. THE BAG SHOWN HERE WAS MADE USING A VARIETY OF DOUBLE KNITTING YARNS, INCLUDING SHINY RIBBON, METALLIC CHAINETTE, NOVELTY YARN, AND SMOOTH WOOL. YOU CAN CHANGE YARN AT THE END OF EVERY ROUND, OR WORK SEVERAL ROUNDS IN THE SAME YARN—THE CHOICE IS UP TO YOU.

YOU WILL NEED

- Double knitting yarns in varying colors and textures—as a guide, to work one round of double crochet at the bag's widest point, you will need about 3yds (3.2m) of yarn
- Size F (4mm) and G (4.5mm) crochet hooks
- Yarn or tapestry needle

GAUGE

Working to an exact gauge is not necessary when making this project.

FINISHED SIZE

Approximately 13in (33cm) deep from top to bottom, 20in (52cm) circumference around widest point, and 13in (33cm) circumference around opening at top.

THE PERFECT KNITTING BAG
Natural fibers do not become charged with static electricity or attract dust. A yarn made from a fiber that does not shed would be perfect for making a storage bag for your crochet and knitting work.

BAG SECTION

The bag is worked from the center of the base. Using size F (4mm) hook, work rounds 1–4 of the double crochet circle motif (see page 77). Continue as follows, changing colors as desired.

ROUND 5: Work as round 4, but work 3 dc between the increases. (80 sts)

ROUND 6: Ch 3, 1 dc into each of next 2 dc, * 2 dc into next dc, 1 dc into each of next 4 dc; rep from * to last 2 dc, 2 dc into next dc, 1 dc into last dc, join with sl st into 3rd of ch 3. (96 sts)

ROUND 7: Ch 1, 1 sc into each dc to end, join with sl st into first sc.

ROUNDS 8–10: Ch 1, 1 sc into each sc to end, join with sl st into first sc.

ROUND 11: Ch 3, sk first sc, 1 dc into each sc to end, join with sl st into 3rd of ch 3.

ROUND 12: Ch 3, sk first dc, 1 dc into each dc to end, join with sl st into 3rd of ch 3.

Continue in the same way without increasing, working either an sc or dc round as follows:

ROUNDS 13, 15, 16, 17, 18, 22 & 23: Work a round of dc.

ROUNDS 14, 19, 20 & 21: Work a round of sc.

ROUND 24: Ch 3, 1 dc into each of next 2 dc, *dc2tog, 1 dc into each of next 4 dc; rep from * to last 3 sts, dc2tog, 1 dc into last dc; join with sl st into 3rd of ch 3. (80 sts)

ROUNDS 25–27: Work a round of dc.

ROUND 28: Ch 3, 1 dc into next dc, *dc2tog, 1 dc into each of next 3 dc; rep from * to last 3 sts, dc2tog, 1 dc into last dc, join with sl st into 3rd of ch 3. (64 sts)

ROUNDS 29–32: Work a round of dc.

ROUND 33: Ch 3, 1 dc into each of next 3 dc, * ch 2, sk next 2 dc, 1 dc into each of next 6 dc; rep from * to last 4 sts, ch 2, sk next 2 dc, 1 dc into each of last 2 dc, join with sl st into 3rd of ch 3.

ROUND 34: Ch 1, 1 sc into first dc, * 1 sc into each of next 2 chs, 1 sc into each of next 6 dc; rep from * to last ch 2 sp, 1 sc into each of next 2 chs, 1 sc into each of next 2 dc, join with sl st into first sc.

ROUNDS 35–40: Work a round of sc.
ROUND 41: Ch 1, sl st into each st to end.
Fasten off yarn.

DRAWSTRINGS (MAKE 2)

Using size G (4.5mm) hook and a smooth yarn,
ch 125 and work a length of single crochet cord
(see page 102).

FINISHING

Weave in the yarn ends (see page 25). If
necessary, press lightly on the wrong side
(see pages 28–29). Thread the two drawstrings
through the holes in the top of the bag, pulling
the ends free at opposite sides of the bag.
Stitch across the short ends of each
drawstring, then weave in the yarn ends.

CHOOSING YARN
Be imaginative with your
choice of yarns when
creating this bag to make
a really unique piece.

CHAPTER FOUR

·····································

Gallery

Drawn from a variety of sources around the world, this chapter features a wide range of crochet garments, accessories, and other items designed to inspire and challenge you with new ideas. Dip into a bounty of color, shape, pattern, and texture and investigate some of the possibilities offered by the wonderful craft of crochet.

◄ **HAPPY PILLOWS**
Ilaria Chiaratti

Variations on the basic granny square (see page 84) are worked in acrylic and wool yarn in a rainbow of colors on unifying white backgrounds for a bright, modern reworking of a well-known traditional design.

CROCHET IN THE HOME

CROCHET IS A VERSATILE TECHNIQUE FOR MAKING HOME ACCESSORIES, PARTICULARLY THOSE ON A LARGE SCALE SUCH AS AFGHANS, BLANKETS, AND THROWS, WHICH CAN EASILY BE MADE IN ONE PIECE. CIRCULAR, SQUARE, AND HEXAGONAL MOTIFS COMBINE WELL TO MAKE PILLOW COVERS AND THROWS THAT WILL ADD INTEREST TO ANY HOME DECOR.

◄ LAYERED CROCHET PILLOW
Rowan Yarns

A layered circle, worked in the round, is expanded to pillow size by working with a large hook and bulky yarn. The harmonious shades of green and blue emphasize the different textures of the various rounds of stitches, and the pillow is finished with a central bright button.

▼ LAMP AND BUNTING
Ilaria Chiaratti

Contrasting bright colors in acrylic/wool yarn are used on a white background for the lampshade, the careful choice of colors giving the granny square (see page 84) a new look. More granny squares are used to make the bunting.

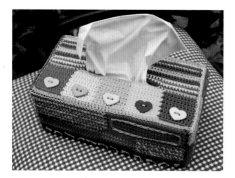

▲ TISSUE BOX COVER
Karin Mijsen

Cotton yarn, worked in single crochet, makes a firm fabric that will keep its shape. Contrasting panels of multicolored stripes (see pages 34–35) and intarsia blocks (see pages 70–71) form the box shape, which is then decorated with surface crochet details (see pages 112–113) and a row of bright buttons.

▲ LACY BOLSTER
Rowan Yarns

Bulky yarn and lacy stitches give an up-to-date look to this bolster. The lacy circles on the ends of the bolster allow the patterned lining to show through, accentuated by the central fabric-covered button.

▲ STOOL COVERS

Ingrid Jansen

These simple stools are made from recycled painted wood, and topped with chunky crochet slipcovers in hard-wearing bulky wool/acrylic/cotton yarn. The contrasting textures of crochet and wood are enhanced by the soft neutral colors.

▲ CHILD'S BEDSPREAD

Ingrid Jansen

Each of the 36 square blocks (see pages 80–84) that form this bedspread is worked with a different color for the lacy circular flower at the center, then completed with a white border. The narrow edging in pink, black, and white is a simple but effective finishing touch.

GARMENTS

CROCHET CAN BE USED TO CREATE A WIDE VARIETY OF GARMENTS, RANGING FROM DELICATE LACY ITEMS FOR EVENING WEAR TO A TRADITIONAL WARM BUT STYLISH SWEATER FOR EVERYDAY USE. CROCHET STITCHES CAN BE WORKED TO A SET PATTERN OR THEY CAN BE EMPLOYED IN A MORE ADVENTUROUS WAY TO MAKE ONE-OF-A-KIND FREEFORM WEARABLES.

▶ LINED BLUE SKIRT
Rowan Yarns

Openwork floral motifs worked in bulky yarn are designed to show the slim-fitting patterned fabric lining that helps the skirt to keep its shape. The ribbed waistband is knitted directly onto the crochet fabric for a slim fit at the waist.

▼ WHITE LACE DRESS
Luanna Perez-Garreaud

Worked in crisp, white cotton yarn, this dress features panels of mesh stitches alternated with panels of lacy circles and trellis patterns (see pages 52–55), and is edged with layers of lacy scallops.

◀ JACKET AND STRIPED SKIRT
Kazekobo (Yoko Hatta)

This orange mohair buttoned jacket, worked in an all-over lace pattern, has elbow-length sleeves, a neat collar, and tie cords trimmed with tassels. The jacket teams perfectly with the slim-fit wool skirt, which is striped in coordinating colors and finished with an interesting tie detail at the waist.

▲ IVORY COTTON DRESS
Kazekobo (Yoko Hatta)

A simple openwork sheath dress, worked in fine ivory cotton, is decorated with elaborate layered flowers (see pages 104–105), leaves, and bunches of grapes in relief, in the manner of traditional Irish crochet lace. This timeless design is bordered with ruffled scallop edgings and lined with ivory silk fabric.

(see pages 60–63)

◀ **MATCHING TOP AND HAT**

Anna Sui, Spring 2011 Collection

The top is created from soft, fuzzy flower motifs joined with crochet chain, teamed with panels of chevron stitch (see pages 60–63) for the yoke and hem. The same flowers are used for the hat, with a scallop border. The clever selection of subtle colors coordinates perfectly with the printed fabric skirt.

▲ **SWEATER DRESS**

Milly by Michelle Smith, Spring 2011 Collection

Part-circles, blocks, and stripes in simple crochet stitches are worked in neutral shades, using black to emphasize the bold geometry of this sweater dress. A touch of gold lurex in the yarn combination adds glamour to the impact.

SCARVES

HIGHLY FASHIONABLE AND POPULAR, CROCHET SCARVES CAN TAKE MANY FORMS, FROM A LACY EVENING ACCESSORY TO A SNUG WINTER WARMER. EXPLORE THE MANY POSSIBLE METHODS OF CONSTRUCTION, FROM USING FREEFORM CROCHET PIECES TO WORKING A LACY STITCH ALL OVER, AND ADDING FRINGES AND TEXTURES.

▲ ▶ PANDA AND REINDEER SCARVES
Jennifer Turco

Basic stitches are worked in the round and cleverly shaped, enabling the designer to give these beasts their individual personalities. The small details, such as toy eyes, embroidered claws, and divided hooves, add the important finishing touches. Made in merino wool, these scarves are both cozy and great fun to wear.

▾ **SPRIAL ROPE SCARF**
De*Nada Designs

This scarf has a most unusual construction—a wide loop worked in double crochet holds a collection of big, bold spirals (see page 103) and tasselled braids of different lengths. The use of a single color throughout emphasizes the contrasting textures.

▴ **MOTIF SCARF**
Rowan Yarns

Large-scale flower motifs of several different designs, worked in the round, form this bold and beautiful scarf. The bulky yarn and soft, pale color show off the details of the stitches.

▲ CREAMY CAPPUCCINO COWL
Maarja Torga

Worked lengthwise in subtle shades of coffee and cream wools, the main section of this cowl is worked in rows of plain stitches, and then edged with elaborate scallops to form a spiral of frothy textures.

◀ DRUID DANCE COWL
Maarja Torga

Heavily textured, multi-shaded bulky wool in a basic stitch is used for the main part of this cowl. Coordinating shades of green are used for the three-dimensional rose trims in finer, smooth yarns.

▲ ROSE RUFFLE SCARF
Maarja Torga

Worked lengthwise in double crochet, this wool scarf begins at the inner edge, with the number of stitches then increased all along the length several times. The outer edge is therefore four or five times longer, forming a deep, luxurious ruffle.

HEAD, NOSE, HANDS, AND TOES

CROCHET IS IDEAL FOR MAKING COZY AND PRACTICAL WINTER HATS AND MITTENS, BUT WHY STOP THERE? A FRILLED EDGE, BOBBLES, TASSELS, OR CORDS CAN TRANSFORM YOUR CREATIONS INTO FUN AND FASHIONABLE ACCESSORIES. EXPLORE THE POSSIBILITIES OFFERED BY NOVELTY YARNS, SUCH AS EYELASH, CHENILLE, BOUCLE, AND MOHAIR, TO ADD TEXTURAL INTEREST TO YOUR CROCHET.

▲ MONSTER EARFLAP HAT
Alessandra Hayden

A child's earflap hat in merino wool takes on a new personality with the addition of bright contrasting scales, multicolored braided ties, and comical features made from appliqué felt.

▲ BEARD BEANIE
Celina Lane

As seen on the ski slopes of Switzerland and at the latest trendy parties, the beard beanie is worked in the round in homespun worsted-weight yarn. The knobbly texture is created with increased and decreased stitches, stacked closely together by working into both the front and back loops of stitches.

▶ PIXIE HAT
Ira Rott

Worked in the round from the point downward, the designer uses worsted-weight yarn and a firm textured stitch to create the unusual shape of this hat. The quirky flower trim (see pages 104–105) is made from toning oddments of various yarns.

◄ **USHANKA**
Lajla Nuhic

The top section of this cozy hat is worked in a blend of mohair and wool, with the lower section and the ties in hand-dyed cotton chenille. The spiral decoration is added in surface crochet (see pages 112–113), firming up the pixie point to help the hat stay in shape.

▼ **ICE LOLLY AND CUPCAKE BOOTEES**
Brigitte Read

Novelty bootees make a great gift for a new baby. The ice lolly bootees are worked in simple stripes of double crochet, with a little cord in single crochet (see pages 102–103) for the stick. The cupcake bootees have a scalloped border on the multicolored frosting, and are finished with a cherry and a little stalk.

▲ **LONG FINGERLESS GLOVES**
Rowan Yarns

These unusual gloves feature a two-row openwork pattern, worked in a repeating sequence of three colors. The use of bulky yarn enlarges the scale of the stitches, making an intriguing multicolored texture.

▶ **JELLY BABY BOOTEES**
Brigitte Read

These little guys are worked throughout in single crochet, with added bobbles (see pages 44–45) for the eyes and noses, and slip stitch for the smiles.

BAGS AND ACCESSORIES

CROCHET IS THE PERFECT MEDIUM FOR MAKING PURSES, BAGS, AND TOTES BECAUSE IT CREATES A STRONG, SUBSTANTIAL FABRIC THAT WILL KEEP ITS SHAPE WELL IN WEAR. WORKED IN THE ROUND OR IN SEPARATE PIECES, A CROCHET BAG PROVIDES THE PERFECT OPPORTUNITY FOR MAKING SMALL-SCALE EXPERIMENTS WITH DIFFERENT YARNS, COLORS, AND TEXTURES.

▲ FLORAL TOTE BAG
Neyya

Floral blocks worked in the round are joined to make this pretty bag and lined with plain blue fabric. The top of the bag and the single crochet handles are finished with a picot edging (see page 99).

▼ CELL PHONE AND IPOD POUCHES
Loretta Grayson

The careful choice of colors makes these little pouches special. Both are worked in merino wool, with one in chevron stripes (see pages 60–63), shading from dark to light blue, and the other in plain stripes (see pages 34–35), shading from bright turquoise through to acid green. Both are finished with chain loops and vintage buttons.

▲ CAT BAG
Carol Ventura

Worked in the round using single crochet, this neat bag is worked in a multicolored crochet technique known as tapestry crochet, which originated in Guatemala and areas of South America.

◄ WATER BOTTLE COZIES
Loretta Grayson

Worked in firm cotton yarn, brightly colored stripes of single crochet chevrons (see pages 60–63) are cleverly finished at the neck of the bottle with a drawstring through the points of the chevrons.

► BASKETWEAVE SHOPPER
Alexandra Feo

Basketweave blocks (see page 67) in strong, bright colors are edged with white single crochet, and seamed together to make this useful shopper. For sturdiness, the top edge and handles are worked in single crochet.

WHIMSY

WHATEVER YOUR FANCY, CROCHET IS THE PERFECT FLEXIBLE MEDIUM FOR EXPERIMENTING WITH CRAZY IDEAS. ALL OF THE DESIGNS INCLUDED HERE USE ONLY SIMPLE, BASIC STITCHES, WHICH ARE EASY TO SHAPE AND MANIPULATE, ALLOWING THE DESIGNERS TO CONCENTRATE ON THE FORM OF EACH PIECE. BE INSPIRED!

▲ BOW TIE

Theodor Sundh

Single crochet rectangles make up this cheerful bow tie, guaranteed to add the finishing touch to any party outfit. One in every color, please!

◄ DAISY WATCH

Luise Roberts

Inspired by childhood daisy chains, the watch strap is worked in fine green crochet cotton with daisies applied on top. Each flower is worked from the center outward in yellow cotton, with petals formed from white cotton chains slip stitched back along their length to the center.

▲ BINKY RABBIT

Dennis Hansbury and Denika Robbins

Binky is a stuffed toy in the Japanese "Amigurumi" style, worked throughout in single crochet for its firmness and ease of shaping. The non-matching eyes and embroidered nose are carefully placed to give Binky the deadpan expression characteristic of the style.

◄ CIRCLE BRACELET

Karin Mijsen

This fun bracelet in jelly bean colors is formed from five interlocking circles worked in smooth cotton yarns. Each circle is composed of several rings covered in single crochet, linked by lengths of chains.

▲ PUG-NACIOUS!
Julie and Bernadette / Sweethoots

One basic hat, three crazy styles—the cactus hat (left) has flyaway ears in single crochet and spikes made from tufts of white eyelash yarn; the fruit hat (upper right) is trimmed with leaves and three-dimensional stuffed fruit; the heart hat (lower right) features stand-up heart ears (worked in the round) and matching red edgings.

▶ MINIATURE CROCHET
Maria Kamenska

Fine cotton yarns and small hooks are used to work these cute pieces in basic stitches. The miniature size is enhanced by the attention given to the tiniest of details, such as the sandal straps and the rose trim on the hat. Both the miniature crochet pieces and the hook are shown at actual size.

CARE OF CROCHET

FOLLOWING A FEW SIMPLE GUIDELINES WHILE YOU ARE WORKING WILL HELP YOU TO KEEP YOUR PIECES OF CROCHET LOOKING FRESH AND CLEAN DURING THE MAKING PROCESS. ONCE A PROJECT IS COMPLETED, IT IS IMPORTANT ALWAYS TO FOLLOW THE YARN MANUFACTURER'S LAUNDERING INSTRUCTIONS AND TO STORE CROCHETED PIECES CAREFULLY AND APPROPRIATELY.

WORKING GUIDELINES

Always wash your hands thoroughly before starting to crochet, and avoid using hand cream because the oils in the cream may transfer to the yarn. When crocheting with light-colored yarns, try to avoid wearing dark-colored garments that shed "bits" while you are working—angora and mohair sweaters are the worst because they shed tiny hairs that get trapped in the crochet. Getting cat and dog hairs on your crochet is also best avoided because they are difficult to remove.

When you have finished making a crochet project, store a small amount of leftover yarn from each project carefully, just in case you need to make repairs in the future. You can wind a length of yarn around a piece of cardboard, making a note of the yarn type and color as well as details of the project. It is also a good idea to attach one of the ball bands from the yarn because this will remind you of the yarn composition, and any special pressing and laundering instructions. File the cards neatly in a dustproof box, and store in a cool, dry place.

LOOKING AFTER CROCHET

Follow the laundering and pressing instructions on the ball band for the particular yarn you have used (for more information on ball bands, see page 22). If the yarn is machine-washable, put the item into a zippered mesh laundry bag to prevent stretching and snagging during the wash cycle. If you do not have a mesh bag, you can use an old, clean white pillowcase instead; simply secure the open end with an elastic ponytail band or work a row of running stitches across the opening to close the pillowcase. If you have household items such as tablecloths or tray cloths trimmed with crochet, treat spills and stains as soon as they occur and repair any damage to the crochet fabric before laundering the item.

For crochet pieces made from yarns that are not machine-washable, wash carefully by hand in hand-hot water with a mild, detergent-free cleaning agent. Most specialist wool or fabric shampoos are ideal, but check that the one you choose does not contain optical brighteners, which will cause yarn colors to fade. Rinse the piece thoroughly in several changes of water at the same temperature as the washing water to avoid felting. Carefully squeeze out as much surplus water as you can, without wringing, then roll the damp item in a towel and press to remove more moisture. Gently ease the item into shape and dry flat, out of direct sunlight. Follow the instructions on the ball band for pressing once the item is dry.

STORING CROCHET

The main enemies of crochet fabrics—apart from dust and dirt—are direct sunlight, which can cause yarn colors to fade and fibers to weaken; excess heat, which makes yarn dry and brittle; damp, which rots fibers; and moths, which can seriously damage woolen yarns. Avoid storing yarns or finished crochet items for any length of time in polythene bags

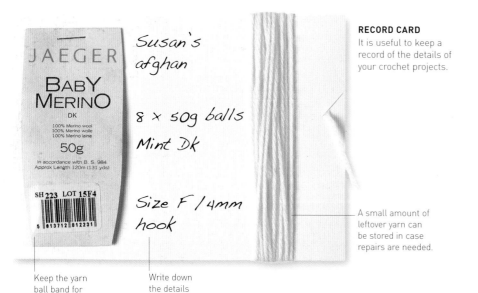

JAEGER
BABY MERINO DK
100% Merino wool
100% Merino wolle
100% Merino laine
50g
In accordance with B. S. 984
Approx Length 120m (131 yds)
SH 223 LOT 15F4

Susan's afghan

8 × 50g balls

Mint Dk

Size F / 4mm hook

Keep the yarn ball band for laundering instructions.

Write down the details of the project.

RECORD CARD
It is useful to keep a record of the details of your crochet projects.

A small amount of leftover yarn can be stored in case repairs are needed.

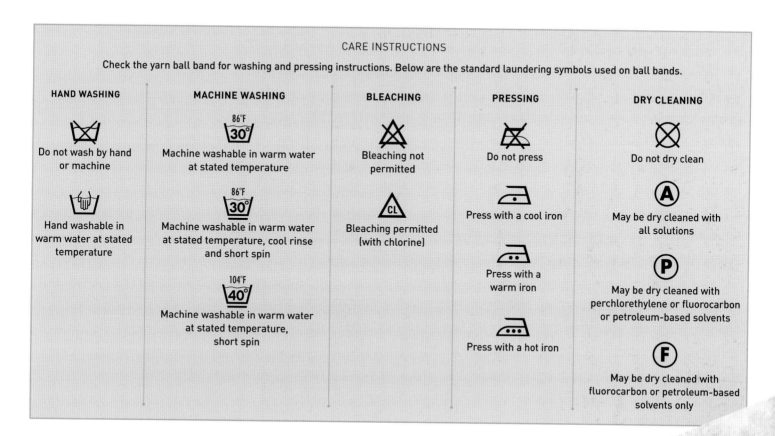

CARE INSTRUCTIONS

Check the yarn ball band for washing and pressing instructions. Below are the standard laundering symbols used on ball bands.

HAND WASHING

Do not wash by hand or machine

Hand washable in warm water at stated temperature

MACHINE WASHING

86°F
30°
Machine washable in warm water at stated temperature

86°F
30°
Machine washable in warm water at stated temperature, cool rinse and short spin

104°F
40°
Machine washable in warm water at stated temperature, short spin

BLEACHING

Bleaching not permitted

CL
Bleaching permitted (with chlorine)

PRESSING

Do not press

Press with a cool iron

Press with a warm iron

Press with a hot iron

DRY CLEANING

Do not dry clean

A
May be dry cleaned with all solutions

P
May be dry cleaned with perchlorethylene or fluorocarbon or petroleum-based solvents

F
May be dry cleaned with fluorocarbon or petroleum-based solvents only

---

because polythene attracts dirt and dust that will transfer readily to your work. Polythene also prevents yarns containing natural fibers such as cotton and linen from breathing, which can result in mildew attacks and eventually weaken or rot the fibers. Instead, store small items by wrapping them in white, acid-free tissue paper or an old cotton pillowcase. For large, heavy items such as winter-weight jackets and sweaters, which might drop and stretch out of shape if stored on coat hangers, fold them loosely between layers of white tissue paper, making sure that each fold is padded with tissue. Store all of the items in a drawer, cupboard, or other dark, dry, moth-free place and check them regularly, refolding larger items. It is also a good idea to make small fabric bags filled with dried lavender flowers and tuck them into the drawer or cupboard with your crochet because the smell deters moths.

STORING PROJECTS

When storing crochet for a long time, wrap it in white, acid-free tissue paper.

ABBREVIATIONS AND SYMBOLS

THESE ARE THE ABBREVIATIONS AND SYMBOLS USED IN THIS BOOK. THERE IS NO WORLDWIDE STANDARD, SO IN OTHER PUBLICATIONS YOU MAY FIND DIFFERENT ABBREVIATIONS AND SYMBOLS.

STANDARD CROCHET ABBREVIATIONS

alt	alternate
beg	beginning
ch(s)	chain(s)
CL	cluster
cont	continue
dc	double crochet
foll	following
hdc	half double crochet
lp(s)	loop(s)
patt	pattern
rem	remaining
rep	repeat
RS	right side
sc	single crochet
sk	skip
sl st	slip stitch
sp(s)	space(s)
st(s)	stitch(es)
tog	together
tr	treble crochet
WS	wrong side
yo	yarn over

STITCH SYMBOLS

Beaded single crochet		Raised double crochet worked around back post	
Bobble		Raised double crochet worked around front post	
Chain		Sequined single crochet	
Cluster		Shell	
Double crochet		Single crochet	
Double crochet into back loop		Single crochet into back loop	
Double crochet into front loop		Single crochet into front loop	
Half double crochet		Slip stitch	
Loop stitch		Spike stitch	
Plain Tunisian stitch		Treble crochet	
Popcorn		Tunisian knit stitch	
Puff stitch		Tunisian mesh stitch	

ADDITIONAL CHART SYMBOLS

Change color	▲▽
Direction of working	→
Do not turn	↱
Fasten off	◀
Foundation row	FR
Join in new color	◁

AMERICAN/ENGLISH TERMINOLOGY

The patterns in this book use American terminology. Patterns published using English terminology can be very confusing because some English terms differ from the American system, as shown below:

American	English
single crochet (sc)	double crochet (dc)
extended single crochet (exsc)	extended double crochet (exdc)
half double crochet (hdc)	half treble crochet (htr)
double crochet (dc)	treble crochet (tr)
treble crochet (tr)	double treble crochet (dtr)
double treble crochet (dtr)	triple treble crochet (trtr or ttr)

ARRANGEMENTS OF SYMBOLS

Description	Symbol	Explanation
Symbols joined at top		A group of symbols may be joined at the top, indicating that these stitches should be worked together as a cluster.
Symbols joined at base		Symbols joined at the base should all be worked into the same stitch below.
Symbols joined at top and bottom		Sometimes a group of stitches is joined at both top and bottom, making a popcorn, bobble, or puff.
Symbols on a curve		Sometimes symbols are drawn along a curve, depending on the construction of the stitch pattern.
Distorted symbols		Some symbols may be lengthened, curved, or spiked to indicate where the hook is inserted below, as for spike stitches.

CATEGORIES OF YARN, GAUGE RANGES, AND RECOMMENDED HOOK SIZES

Below are the most commonly used gauges and needle or hook sizes for specific yarn categories.

Yarn weight category	Super fine	Fine	Light	Medium	Bulky	Super bulky
Type of yarns in category	Sock, fingering, baby	Sport, baby	DK, light worsted	Worsted, afghan, aran	Chunky, craft, rug	Bulky, roving
Crochet gauge ranges in single crochet to 4in (10cm)	21–32 sts	16–20 sts	12–17 sts	11–14 sts	8–11 sts	5–9 sts
Recommended hook in metric size range	2.25–3.5mm	3.5–4.5mm	4.5–5.5mm	5.5–6.5mm	6.5–9mm	9mm and larger
Recommended hook in US size range	B–1 to E–4	E–4 to 7	7 to I–9	I–9 to K–10½	K–10½ to M–13	M–13 and larger

CROCHET HOOKS
Crochet hooks are available in a wide range of sizes, shapes, and materials.

Super fine

Medium

Bulky

Fine

Light

Super bulky

YARN WEIGHTS
It is not always possible to guess a yarn weight from simply looking at a strand of yarn.

GLOSSARY

BALL BAND
The paper strip or paper tag on a ball or skein of yarn. A ball band gives information about weight, shade number, dye lot number, and fiber content of the yarn. It may also show care instructions and other details, including yardage and suggested gauge and hook size.

BLOCKING
Setting a piece of crochet by stretching and pinning it out on a flat surface before steaming or treating with cold water.

BOBBLE
Several stitches worked in the same place and joined together at the top to make a decorative raised bump. Bobbles are often worked on a background of shorter stitches.

BORDER
A decorative strip of crochet, usually deep with one straight and one shaped edge, that is used for trimming pieces of crochet or fabric.

BRAID
A narrow, decorative strip of crochet similar in appearance to a purchased furnishing braid.

BROOMSTICK CROCHET
A particular type of crochet that is worked with both a crochet hook and a "broomstick" such as a large knitting needle.

CHAIN SPACE
Space formed by working lengths of chain stitches between other stitches. Also known as chain loops or chain arches.

CLUSTER
Several incomplete stitches worked together so that they join at the top.

DECREASE
Removing one or more stitches to reduce the number of working stitches.

DYE LOT
The batch of dye used for a specific ball of yarn. Shades can vary between batches, so use yarn from the same dye lot to make an item.

EDGE FINISH
A decorative crochet edging worked directly onto the edge of a piece of crochet.

EDGING
A decorative trim applied to the edges of a crochet or woven fabric. Crochet edgings can either be worked separately and then sewn on (such as a border), or they can be worked directly onto the crochet fabric (an edge finish).

FAN
Several stitches worked into the same chain or stitch to create a fan or shell shape.

FIBER
Natural or synthetic substances spun together to make yarn.

FILET CROCHET
A type of crochet based on a regular mesh grid, with certain holes filled by extra stitches to form a pattern. Filet crochet is usually worked from a chart rather than written instructions.

FOUNDATION CHAIN
A length of chain stitches that forms the base for a piece of crochet.

FOUNDATION ROW
In a stitch pattern, the first row worked into the foundation chain. The foundation row is not repeated as part of the pattern.

GAUGE
The looseness or tightness of a crochet fabric expressed as a specific number of stitches and rows in a given area, usually 4in (10cm) square, with a suggested hook size.

HEADING
Extra rows of plain crochet worked on the long straight edge of an edging or border to add strength and durability.

INCREASE
Adding one or more stitches to increase the number of working stitches.

INSERTION
A narrow, decorative strip of crochet, similar to braid, that is sewn between two pieces of fabric.

INTARSIA
Intarsia produces a design featuring areas of different colors that are each worked with a separate small ball of yarn. Intarsia patterns are worked in two or more colors from a colored chart on a grid. Each colored square on the chart represents one stitch.

JACQUARD
Jacquard patterns appear similar to intarsia, but the yarns are carried along the row rather than being used separately. This produces a slightly denser fabric if worked with the same hook size as that used for the same pattern worked in intarsia. A jacquard pattern is shown as a colored chart on a grid. Each colored square on the chart represents one stitch.

LACE
A stitch pattern forming an openwork design similar in appearance to lace fabric.

MESH
An open stitch pattern forming a regular geometric grid.

MOTIF
A shaped piece of crochet, often worked in rounds. Several motifs can be joined together rather like fabric patchwork to make a larger piece. Also known as a medallion or block.

PATTERN
A set of instructions showing exactly how to make a garment or other crochet item.

PATTERN REPEAT
The specific number of rows or rounds that are needed to complete one stitch pattern.

PICOT
A decorative chain space often closed into a ring with a slip stitch. The number of chains in a picot can vary.

PLY
A single strand of yarn made by twisting fibers together. Most yarn is made from two or more plies twisted together to make different yarn weights, although some woolen yarns are made from a single thick ply.

PUFF
Several half double crochet stitches worked in the same place, and joined together at the top to make a raised stitch.

RIGHT SIDE
The front of crochet fabric. This side is usually visible on a finished item, although some stitch patterns may be reversible.

ROUND
A row of crochet worked in the round; the end of one round is joined to the beginning of the same round. Rounds of crochet can form flat motifs or tubular shapes.

ROW
A line of stitches worked from side to side to make a flat piece of crochet.

SEAM
The join made where two pieces of crochet are stitched or crocheted together.

SEWING NEEDLE
A needle with a sharp point used for applying a crochet braid, edging, or border to a piece of fabric.

SPIKE
A decorative stitch worked by inserting the hook from front to back of the work, one or more rows below the normal position, and/or to the right or left of the working stitch.

STARTING CHAIN
A specific number of chain stitches worked at the beginning of a round to bring the hook up to the correct height for the next stitch that is being worked.

STITCH PATTERN
A sequence or combination of crochet stitches that is repeated over and over again to create a piece of crochet fabric.

SURFACE CROCHET
Rows of decorative crochet worked on top of a crochet background.

SYMBOL CHART
A chart that describes a crochet pattern visually, using symbols to indicate the different stitches and exactly where and how they should be placed in relation to one another.

TAPESTRY NEEDLE
A large, blunt-ended embroidery needle used for sewing pieces of crochet together.

TRIM
A length of crochet worked separately and sewn onto a main piece, or onto plain fabric, as a decoration.

TUNISIAN CROCHET
A type of crochet worked with a special long hook. Tunisian crochet is worked back and forth in rows without turning the work.

TURNING CHAIN
A specific number of chain stitches worked at the beginning of a row to bring the hook up to the correct height for the next stitch that is being worked.

WRONG SIDE
The reverse side of crochet fabric. This side is not usually visible on a finished item.

YARN NEEDLE
A blunt-ended needle with a large eye used for sewing pieces of crochet together.

SUPPLIERS

MIDWEST

ILLINOIS
Knit 1
Chicago, IL 60613
773-244-1646
www.knit1chgo.com

Sunflower Samplings
Crystal Lake, IL 60014
815-455-2919

INDIANA
Mass. Ave. Knit Shop
Indianapolis, IN 46203
317-638-1833
www.massaveknitshoponline.com

River Knits Fine Yarns
Lafayette, IN 47901
765-742-5648
www.riverknitsyarns.com

IOWA
The Knitting Shoppe
Iowa City, IA 52240
319-337-4920
www.theknittingshoppeic.com

Three Oaks Knits
Waterloo, IA 50701
319-883-8000
www.threeoaksknits.com

KANSAS
Wildflower Yarns and Knitwear
Manhattan, KS 66502
785-537-1826
www.wildflowerknits.com

Yarn Barn
Lawrence, KS 66044
785-842-4333
www.yarnbarn-ks.com

MICHIGAN

City Knits
Detroit, MI 48045
313-872-9665
www.cityknits.com

Knit a Round Yarn Shop
Ann Arbor, MI 48105
734-998-3771
www.knitaround.com

The Wool and the Floss
Grosse Point, MI 48230
313-882-9110
www.thewoolandthefloss.net

MINNESOTA

Linden Hills Yarn
Minneapolis, MN 55410
612-929-1255
www.lindenhillsyarn.com

3 Kittens Needle Arts
Mendota Heights, MN 55118
651-457-4969
www.3kittensneedlearts.com

MISSOURI

True Blue Fiber Friends
Columbia, MO 65203
573-443-8233
www.truebluefiberfriends.com

Simply Fibers
Springfield, MO 65807
417-881-9276
www.simplyfibers.com

NEBRASKA

Personal Threads Boutique
Omaha, NE 68114
402-391-7733
www.personalthreads.com

The Plum Nelly
Hastings, NE 68901
402-462-2490
www.theplumnelly.com

NORTH DAKOTA

Prairie Yarns
Fargo, ND 58103
701-280-1478
www.prairieyarns.com

OHIO

Fiberlicious
Cincinnati, OH 45243
513-561-8808
www.fiberlicious.com

Fine Points
Cleveland, OH 44120
216-229-6644
www.finepoints.com

SOUTH DAKOTA

Ben Franklin
Mitchell, SD 57301
605-990-2500
www.benfranklin.com

Athena Fibers
Sioux Falls, SD 57105
605-271-0741
www.athenafibers.com

WISCONSIN

Monterey Yarn
Green Bay, WI 54311
920-884-5258
www.montereyyarn.com

Ruhama's Yarn & Needlepoint
Whitefish Bay, WI 53217
414-332-2660
www.ruhamas.com

NORTHEAST

CONNECTICUT

Mystic River Yarns
Mystic, CT 06355
860-536-4305
www.mysticriveryarns.com

Yarns Down Under
Deep River, CT 06417
860-526-9986
www.yarnsdownunder.com

DELAWARE

Knit2purl2
Newark, DE 19711
302-737-4917
www.knit2purl2.com

MAINE

KnitWit Yarn Shop
Portland, ME 04101
207-774-6444

The Fiber Cottage
Waldo, ME 049153
207-342-2378
www.thefibercottage.com

MASSACHUSETTS

Wild and Woolly Studio
Lexington, MA 02420
781-861-7717
www.wildandwoollystudio.com

Windsor Button
Boston, MA 02111
617-482-4969
www.windsorbutton.com

NEW JERSEY

Wooly Monmouth
Red Bank, NJ 07701
732-224-9276
www.woolymonmouth.com

Woolbearers
Mount Holly, NJ 08060
609-914-0003
www.woolbearers.com

NEW HAMPSHIRE

Charlotte's Web
Exeter, NH 03833
888-244-6460
www.charlotteswebyarns.com

The Elegant Ewe
Concord, NH 03301
603-226-0066
www.elegantewe.com

NEW YORK

Downtown Yarns
New York, NY 10009
212-995-5991
www.downtownyarns.com

Lion Brand Yarn Studio
New York, NY 10011
212-243-9070
www.lionbrandyarnstudio.com

Purl Soho
New York, NY 10013
212-420-8796
www.purlsoho.com

Knit One Needlepoint Too
Monticello, NY 12701
845-791-5648
www.k1n2.com

PENNSYLVANIA

Knitter's Dream
Harrisburg, PA 17112
717-599-7665
www.knittersdream.com

Loop Yarn
Philadelphia, PA 19146
215-893-9939
www.loopyarn.com

Natural Stitches
Pittsburgh, PA 15206
412-441-4410
www.naturalstitches.com

RHODE ISLAND

Fresh Purls
Providence, RI 02906
401-270-8220
www.freshpurls.com

The Yarn Outlet
Pawtucket, RI 02860
401-722-5600
www.theyarnoutlet.com

VERMONT

Pine Ledge Fiber Studio
Fairfax, VT 05454
802-849-2876
www.pineledge.com

Whippletree Yarn Shop
Woodstock, VT 05091
802-432-1198
www.whippletreeyarn.com

PACIFIC

ALASKA

Changing Threads
Skagway, AK 99840
907-983-3700
www.changingthreads.com

A Weaver's Yarn
Fairbanks, AK 99709
907-374-1995
www.aweaversyarn.com

CALIFORNIA

Trendsetter Yarns
Van Nuys, CA 91406
818-780-5497
www.trendsetteryarns.com

Wildfiber
Santa Monica, CA 90404
310-458-2748
www.wildfiber.com

Jennifer Knits
Los Angeles, CA 90049
310-471-8733
www.jenniferknits.com

HAWAII

Yarn Story
Honolulu, HI 96814
808-593-2212
www.yarnstoryhawaii.com

OREGON

Knit Shop
Eugene, OR 97405
541-434-0430
www.knit-shop.com

The Naked Sheep Knit Shop
Portland, OR 97217
503-283-2004
www.thenakedsheepknitshop.com

WASHINGTON

Acorn Street Shop
Seattle, WA 98105
206-525-1726
www.acornstreet.com

Amanda's Art Yarns
Poulsbo, WA 98370
360-779-3666

SOUTH

ALABAMA

Memory Hagler Knitting
Birmingham, AL 35216
205-822-7875
www.knithappenz.com

ARKANSAS

The Yarn Mart
Little Rock, AR 72207
501-666-6505
www.theyarnmart.com

FLORIDA

Elegant Stitches
Miami, FL 33176
305-232-4005
www.elegant-stitches.com

Knit 'n Knibble
Tampa, FL 33611
813-837-5648
www.knitnknibble.com

GEORGIA

The Knitting Emporium
Kennesaw, GA 30144
770-421-1919
www.knittingemporium.com

KENTUCKY

The Stitche Niche
Lexington, KY 40503
859-277-2604

LOUISIANA

Yarn Nook
Lafayette, LA 70503
337-593-8558
www.yarnnook.com

MARYLAND

Woolworks
Baltimore, MD 21209
410-337-2060
www.woolworksbalt.com

MISSISSIPPI

The Knit Studio
Jackson, MI 39110
601-991-3092
www.theknitstudio.com

NORTH CAROLINA

Knit One Smock Too
Winston Salem, NC 27104
336-765-9099
www.knitonesmocktoo.
blogspot.com

OKLAHOMA

The Gourmet Yarn Co.
Oklahoma City, OK 73120
405-286-3737
www.gourmetyarnco.com

Stitches
Tulsa, OK 74105
918-747-8838
www.stitchesoftulsa.com

SOUTH CAROLINA

Island Knits
Pawleys Island, SC 29585
843-235-0110
www.islandknit.com

Knit
Charleston, SC 29401
843-937-8500
www.knitk.com

TENNESSEE

The Yarn Studio
Memphis, TN 38112
901-335-4380
www.yarnstudio.com

TEXAS

Desert Designs Knitz
Dallas, TX 75254
972-392-9276
www.desertdesigns.knitz.com

Hill Country Weavers
Austin, TX 78704
512-707-7396
www.hillcountryweavers.com

Nimble Fingers
Houston, TX 77024
713-722-7244
www.nimblefingerstx.com

VIRGINIA

The Knitting Basket
Richmond, VA 23226
804-282-2909
www.theknittingbasket.biz

Knitting Sisters
Williamsburg, VA 23185
757-258-5005
www.knittingsisters.com

WASHINGTON, DC

Stitch DC, Inc.
Washington, DC 20016
202-487-4337
www.stitchdc.com

WEST VIRGINIA

Kanawha City Yarn Company
Charleston, WV 25304
304-926-8589
www.kcyarnco.com

WEST

ARIZONA

The Tuscon Yarn Company
Tucson, AZ 85704
520-229-9276
www.tucsonyarn.com

COLORADO

Showers of Flowers Yarn Shop
Lakewood, CO 80214
303-233-2525
www.showersofflowers.com

Shuttles, Spindles & Skeins
Boulder, CO 80305
303-494-1071
www.shuttlesspindles
andskeins.com

Lamb Shoppe
Denver, CO 80206
303-322-2223
www.thelambshoppe.com

IDAHO

The Yarn Shoppe
Meridian, ID 83642
208-884-4885
www.the-yarn-shop.com

MONTANA

Knit 'n Needle
Whitefish, MT 59937
406-862-6390
www.knitandneedle.com

Pam's Knit 'n' Stitch
Great Falls, MT 59401
406-761-4652
www.pamsknitnstitch.com

NEVADA

Gail Knits
Las Vegas, NV 89117
702-838-7713
www.gailknits.com

Wooly Wonders
Las Vegas, NV 89121
702-547-1661
www.woolywonders.com

NEW MEXICO

Village Wools
Albuquerque, NM 87113
505-883-2919
www.villagewools.com

UTAH

Heindselman's Yarn,
Needlework, and Gifts
Provo, UT 84601
801-373-5193

Judy's Novelty Wool
Centerville, UT 84014
801-298-1356
www.judysnoveltywool.com

Blazing Needles
Salt Lake City, UT 84105
801-487-5648
www.blazing-needles.com

WYOMING

Cowgirl Yarn
Laramie, WY 82070
307-755-9276
www.cowgirlyarn.com

Over the Moon
Sheridan, WY 82801
307-673-5991

ADDITIONAL WEB RESOURCES

The Craft Yarn Council: www.craftyarncouncil.com
The Crochet Guild of America: www.crochet.org

SELECTED SUPPLIERS
www.buy-mail.co.uk
www.cascadeyarns.com
www.coatscrafts.co.uk
www.colourway.co.uk
www.coolwoolz.co.uk
www.crystalpalaceyarns.com
www.designeryarns.uk.com
www.diamondyarns.com
www.ethknits.co.uk
www.e-yarn.com
www.hantex.co.uk
www.hook-n-needle.com
www.kangaroo.uk.com
www.karpstyles.ca
www.knitrowan.com
   (features worldwide list of stockists of Rowan yarns)
www.knittersdream.com
www.knittingfever.com
www.knitwellwools.co.uk
www.lacis.com
www.maggiescrochet.com
www.mcadirect.com
www.patternworks.com
www.patonsyarns.com
www.personalthreads.com
www.ravelry.com
www.sakonnetpurls.com
www.shetlandwoolbrokers.co.uk
www.sirdar.co.uk
www.spiningayarn.co.uk
www.theknittinggarden.com
www.upcountry.co.uk
www.yarncompany.com
www.yarnexpressions.com
www.yarnmarket.com

INDEX

Page numbers in *italic* refer to pattern instructions in the stitch collections

CREDITS

Quarto would like to thank the following designers for kindly supplying images reproduced in this book. Designers are acknowledged beside their work featured in the gallery.

- Ilaria Chiaratti: www.idainteriorlifestyle.blogspot.com
- Rowan Yarns: www.knitrowan.com, 01484 681 881
- De*Nada Designs: www.denadadesign.com
- Alexandra Feo (pattern and photography): www.madamecraft.com
- Loretta Grayson: www.rettg.blogspot.com
- Dennis Hansbury and Denika Robbins
- Alessandra Hayden: www.justbehappycrochet.com
- Ingrid Jansen: www.woodwoolstool.com (Ingrid's work is also featured on page 32)
- Julie and Bernadette / Sweethoots: www.sweethoots.etsy.com
- Maria Kamenska: www.MariaKonstantin.etsy.com
- Kazekobo (Yoko Hatta): www.kazekobo.net
- Celina Lane: www.SimplyCollectible.etsy.com
- Karin Mijsen: www.karinaandehaak.blogspot.com (Karin's work is also featured on pages 2–3)
- Lajla Nuhic: www.lajla.ca
- Luanna Perez-Gareaud
- Brigitte Read from Roman Sock: www.littlegreen.typepad.com
- Ira Rott: www.irarott.com
- Theodor Sundh: www.crochetbloke.blogspot.co.uk
- Maarja Torga: www.WhisperTwister.etsy.com
- Jennifer Turco: www.beeskneesknitting.com
- Carol Ventura: www.tapestrycrochet.com

Quarto would also like to acknowledge the following:
- Pages 4 & 138: Nata Pupo / Shutterstock.com (www.annasui.com & www.millyny.com)
- Page 144: Neyya / istockphoto.com

Thanks also to the models, Isabelle Crawford and Kryssy Moss, and to Betty Barnden for writing the gallery captions.

All other photographs and illustrations are the copyright of Quarto Publishing plc. While every effort has been made to credit contributors, Quarto would like to apologize should there have been any omissions or errors—and would be pleased to make the appropriate correction for future editions of the book.